Daily Enneagram Reflections
— with journal prompts —

Your 90-Day Journey Towards More Harmony,
Joy, and Mental Clarity

by Jody and Jeff Sanders

Table of Contents

Introduction: Your Next 90 Days

Time is a funny concept. Each day can feel gruelingly long, but three months seem to go by in the blink of an eye. Day after day, it's so easy to move through life the same way we always have. Think about yourself three months ago. What were you doing? Is your life dramatically different today? If not, don't worry – the vast majority of people don't make profound life-improvements each week, so it's perfectly normal to look back and notice that the you of three months ago is pretty much the same you of today.

We can wake up every single morning and trudge through each day the same way we always have and in months, we would be exactly where we are right now: the same person, with the same psychological hang-ups, tripping over the same insecurities, fears, and blind spots that we always have.

It would be so very easy to keep on marching along our familiar life paths, but you know what? It's also easy to reject the idea of stagnation and grow a tiny little bit every single day.

Today, you've elected to level-up beyond what's "normal" and take control of your most powerful asset: your mind. Over the next 90 days, you will spend about 10-15 minutes each day bringing the automatic thought patterns that covertly rule your life into broad daylight. When you shine a light onto your autopilot behaviors, you can critically decide if those patterns are helping, hurting, or not doing anything in particular for you.

With that knowledge, you can cherry-pick which ones to keep, which ones to alter ever-so-slightly, and which ones to axe completely. That might sound like a lot of heavy psychological lifting, and it would be – *if* we weren't here to guide you every step of the way. But here we are, ready to embark on this 90-day journey with you! So how will we do it?

This seems like a great time to introduce ourselves! Hi, our names are Jody and Jeff Sanders. We are life-long students of the Enneagram, an ancient tool for understanding human personality that has stood the test of time because of its uncanny ability to precisely classify human behavior, predict how particular personalities behave when under stress and when thriving, and anticipate how people of different personalities will interact with each other. In short, it's a personality typing system, but its roots are very long. Here, we'll give you the cliffnotes version, but if you want more, we wrote two books that explain it in great depth. Go to www.personalityintel.com to see our collection or, if you prefer the free variety, email us to see if there are any spots available in our *Enneagram Insiders VIP Club*. After joining, we'll send you free, advance access to our books in exchange for your honest feedback. Email us at jjsanders@personalityintel.com to learn more.

"Enneagram" means "nine writings" (ennea/nine, gram/a thing written), because it is a graphical representation of nine different ways of being and thinking.

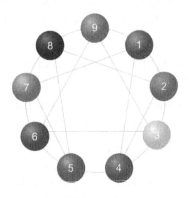

You might hear people say they are a Type 1, or a Type 2, etc. This means that that number point on the Enneagram is their dominant personality type and defines most of their habitual thoughts and actions. Each person is a unique blend of **all** nine points on the Enneagram, so while it might be tempting to label yourself with one Enneagram point in particular and disregard the others, you'll become your best self only when you explore all aspects of how our minds tend to operate. You can spend a little extra time on the points that make up the bulk of your personality, but its critical to make sure each point gets attention. To ensure this, our 90-day journey will be broken up into nine blocks of 10 days each. Each block will be devoted to an Enneagram point, starting from Point 1 and progressing until Point 9.

Each Enneagram point has a **vice** and a **virtue**. If you are familiar with the 7 deadly sins, you'll recognize most of the vices.

The 9 Vices

Point 1:   Anger
Point 2:   Pride
Point 3:   Deceit
Point 4:   Envy
Point 5:   Avarice
Point 6:   Fear
Point 7:   Gluttony
Point 8:   Lust
Point 9:   Sloth

All of these vices show up in our lives. But hey, we are decent people, right? We wouldn't be embarking on a 90-day journey if we didn't really care about being the best version of ourselves. Surely, these vices can't be ruling, *our* lives, right? Wrong, unfortunately. These vices are sneaky! They show up in ways we would never expect if we didn't specifically go looking for them.

On our 90-day journey, we will focus on each Enneagram Point's *virtue*. For every vice, there is a virtue. Gaining more of a given point's virtue will naturally diffuse its vice. Gaining more serenity, for example, will naturally diffuse anger in your life. And gaining more humility will naturally diffuse pride.

The 9 Virtues		Days
Point 1:	Serenity	Days 1-10
Point 2:	Humility	Days 11-20
Point 3:	Authenticity	Days 21-30
Point 4:	Equanimity	Days 31-40
Point 5:	Non-Attachment	Days 41-50
Point 6:	Courage	Days 51-60
Point 7:	Sobriety	Days 61-70
Point 8:	Innocence	Days 71-80
Point 9:	Action	Days 81-90

To get you into the right frame of mind before starting each new block, you will begin each one with a 10-minute meditation. This means we will complete nine meditations spread out over the course of our 90 days together. Again, we will be here to guide you through this! Before you move on, get our free guided meditations at: www.personalityintel.com/meditations.

For each day in the block, you'll read and reflect on a short passage. Then, you'll be prompted through two short journal entries that will help you synthesize the information and personalize it for you.

When you break it down, it's a very simple process!

Step 1: at the beginning of every block, engage in a 10-minute meditation
Step 2: during each day of the block, read a short passage and complete 2 journal prompts

Before we finally jump in, there's one last thing that is very important. This journey will only work if you stay on the path. It will only take 10-15 minutes each day to see massive results at the end of three months, but it is important you actually commit to pull out this book with a pen in hand each day for the next 90-days. If you don't make the commitment now, it will be easy to just let it "happen when it happens." We all know what transpires after that: we get excited for a few days and go strong, but then we start to forget a couple of times each week, until this book is collecting dust on a shelf somewhere. A simple commitment contract can change that. Studies show if you put your goals in writing and formalize them, you significantly increase your chance of following through. It works better if you have a witness, so we'll sign too and be your virtual witnesses! [If you want us to follow up with you in real time, feel free to send us an email. We love hearing from you and can be reached at: jjsanders@personalityintel.com].

Here and now, make the commitment. Try to also specify when and where you will stick this new habit into your daily routine (e.g., in the morning while on the bus commuting to work) and what you will reward yourself with once you complete the commitment in full. Write out the following commitment contract on the lines below:

I, <<your name>> commit to spend 10-15 minutes on my Enneagram journey each day. I will fill out this daily reader <<when/where>>. Once I complete the 90 days, I will reward myself with <<the reward you selected>>.

Date: _____

Your Signature: _____

Witness Signatures:

Jody Sanders

Jeff Sanders

---

se·ren·i·ty

/səˈrenədē/

noun

the state of being calm, peaceful, and untroubled

---

day 1

Healthy striving is self-focused: How can I improve?
Perfectionism is other-focused: What will they think?

Brené Brown

The title of "perfectionist' has become romanticized. Society equates "perfectionist" with "hard worker" and "high achiever." Working for more hours and sleeping for less won't necessarily make you more productive, but it might make you look successful and ambitious. However, "perfectionism" isn't so much an honorable accolade as it is a shield from unpleasant feelings. When we strive to be perfect, we're striving to avoid judgment, shame, and criticism. Perfectionism is a way to convince ourselves that we are living up to a high moral and ethical standard. If we are struggling to be perfect, we're really struggling to prove to ourselves that we are "good" or "right."

The reality is that you can work hard on yourself and be high-achieving while still believing that you are good and worthy. You can accept that you are good and worthy while still falling short of your goals and expectations. Failure doesn't make you "bad." In fact, failure is a part of growth. And the more you choose to improve and grow yourself, the less you'll feel the impulse to judge and criticize yourself.

1. Think of a time you "failed" or were imperfect. What growth came out of that experience?

_____

_____

_____

_____

_____

_____

_____

2. When do you most doubt whether you are good or worthy enough?

_____

_____

_____

_____

_____

_____

_____

————— ” —————

Embrace being perfectly imperfect. Learn from your mistakes and forgive yourself, you'll be happier.

Roy Bennett

There's only one thing in the world we are sure to be perfect at: being imperfect. No matter how hard we try, there's always room for improvement. But if we always think like that, we'll drive ourselves crazy. Not only are we guaranteed to be imperfect and make mistakes, but we are also guaranteed endless opportunities to learn from our mistakes if we choose to accept them.

When it comes to making mistakes, it's all too easy to let fear take over. Instead of seeing mistakes and imperfections as openings, we see them as problems. Today, look at mistakes as an opportunity for growth rather than an obstacle to overcome. By changing your perception of what mistakes really are, you can embrace them as part of the learning process. Remember: progress is never linear. Mistakes, setbacks, and problems make up the lifelong journey of progress. Don't let your fear of messing up get in the way of your growth. By allowing yourself the grace to mess up and giving yourself the compassion to continue, you'll be opening endless doors for joy and growth.

1. What mistakes are you afraid of making?

_____

_____

_____

_____

_____

_____

2. What do you stand to lose by making those mistakes? What do you stand to gain?

_____

_____

_____

_____

_____

_____

_____

day 3

The more I expect, the more unhappy I am going to be.
The more I accept, the more serene I am.

Michael J. Fox

We all have expectations. We expect our alarms to go off in the morning, we expect to get to work on time, and we expect to have a break during the day. But imagine a day when it all goes wrong: you miss your alarm, traffic is terrible, and you are so busy that you don't get a chance to sit down. How does a day feel when the reality of the day falls short of your expectations? Expectations are a surefire way to run into disappointment and resentment.

Instead of expecting your day to go a certain way or expecting your friends and family to behave one way or another, choose to accept the realities of daily life. Accept the mistakes and inconveniences for what they are: an unavoidable part of life. From there, you can also choose to see the joy in the unexpected or undesirable. Being frustrated with heavy traffic won't make you get anywhere any faster, but it could give you more time to listen to your favorite music or an audiobook. Your day might be uncomfortably busy, but that will make the time you find rest even more relieving. Expectations are a set-up for frustration, but accepting frustrations opens the door for joy and peace.

1. What expectations do you have in your life that are frustrating when unmet?

_____

_____

_____

_____

_____

_____

2. Which parts of your daily life can you accept to bring yourself more serenity?

_____

_____

_____

_____

_____

_____

———————————— " ————————————

You can't always control what goes on outside. But you can always control what goes on inside.

Wayne Dyer

Have you ever had an imaginary discussion or argument with someone in your head? Maybe you thought of the perfect response to a comment or event hours after the fact. Imagined scenarios are cathartic because we have full control over the narrative. In our imaginations, we always have the appropriate response because we control the script. However, we also know that real-life isn't scripted and we can't control, or even predict, what happens in our surroundings.

Of course, you can't have a discussion or argument with another person and have it go according to the script in your head. But you can always prepare yourself to handle the world, no matter how unpredictable, with grace and dignity. People don't often follow our scripts or our expectations, but we can always choose to act and respond according to what we feel is right. Today, practice allowing yourself to let go of your expectations for people and situations and focus on your own autonomy. You can't control what goes on around you, but you have full power over yourself.

1. What situation in your life are you trying to control that you don't have real power over?

_____

_____

_____

_____

_____

_____

2. How can you respond to unpredictable situations in a way that is true to yourself?

_____

_____

_____

_____

_____

_____

_____

day 5

Do not let the behavior of others destroy your inner peace.

Dalai Lama

People can really ruin a day, if you let them. They can also ruin more than a day, if you allow their behavior to dictate your own. All people, just as much as you do, have the autonomy to act and behave however they want. Often it isn't a problem, but other times it can get in the way of your own inner peace. The only person you are in constant company with is yourself. So make sure you are the only one responsible for your mood.

If you've ever allowed, for example, a coworker's rude words or the bad behavior of a stranger to leave a lasting mark on your day, you allowed someone else to control your peace. Remember that you can control what goes on in your head, but not in anyone else's. Let go of your expectations for others' behaviors and allow yourself to act in whichever way is true to you. The most important and powerful action you can take for yourself is maintaining ownership of your peace and happiness. No one can take that from you, as long as you don't allow it.

1. What behaviors in others disrupt your peace?

_____

_____

_____

_____

_____

_____

2. How can you change your reaction or feelings to maintain your peace?

_____

_____

_____

_____

_____

_____

day 6

———————— ” ————————

Patience is the calm acceptance that things can happen in a different order than the one you have in mind.

David G. Allen

List-keeping, plan-making individuals often have an idea of how and in which order parts of their lives will go. Whether it's as ordinary as expecting a cup of coffee before work or as life-changing as expecting to fall in love before a certain age, it's common to imagine an order of events in our lives. However, it's also common for people to be frustrated and impatient when their lives don't move according to their imagined plan. The antidote to this poisonous behavior is as simple as it is difficult: patience.

Life tends to give and take away when it wants to – with little regard to what we imagine. We can take steps to make events happen for ourselves, but ultimately, life unfolds how it's going to whether we are ready for it or not. Instead of being anxious about imagined timelines, allow events to happen as they will. Patience gives us the serenity to experience life in the moment rather than angsting about what has or has not happened yet. You will have your coffee and you will fall in love, but give yourself the space to let it happen on its own schedule.

1. Do you have an order of events for your life? What does it look like?

_____

_____

_____

_____

_____

_____

2. How can you practice patience in your life today?

_____

_____

_____

_____

_____

_____

day 7

Tell that imperious voice in your head to be still.

Barbara Kingsolver

We all have an inner critic. Some have a quiet and polite voice in their head. Others, however, are plagued by a louder and harsher inner critic. If you find yourself afraid to make changes, get nervous about making mistakes, or get worried about what others think of you, you may have a loud, domineering inner critic.

Luckily, you have control over your inner critic – even when it feels like it has control over you. Take charge: when the voice in your head says you're not good enough or important enough or smart enough, tell it to be quiet! Challenge the nasty things it says about you. If it warns you that a task will be too hard, remind it of every challenge you have already overcome. When it tells you that you are not brave enough, tell it that you have made it this far. You are living, breathing proof that you have what it takes to live your life. You don't need to believe the harsh words your inner critic speaks. Tell it to be quiet and do what you know you can do.

1. How often does your inner critic limit you?

_____

_____

_____

_____

_____

_____

2. List some positive thoughts you can use to challenge your inner critic.

_____

_____

_____

_____

_____

_____

_____

day 8

Do your work, then step back. The only path to serenity.

Lao Tzu

Think of the most beautiful piece of art you've ever seen, the most moving book you've ever read, or the most delicious meal you've ever eaten. All of them have something in common: each was work done by someone who finished it for you to enjoy. Imagine if the artist hadn't been satisfied, or if the author was unwilling to share her story, or if the chef second-guessed his ingredient choices.

We could continue working on our projects and hobbies until we think they are perfect. But wouldn't it bother you to never finish something because you were constantly tweaking it? If you have perfectionist tendencies, you may be tempted to continuously tweak and adjust whatever you are working on. But where's the sense of peace and finality in finishing a project if you never get around to finishing it? Instead of revisiting past work in attempts to polish and perfect, learn to recognize when something is "done." Whether you've reached the deadline, a project is technically complete, or it's in someone else's hands. Do your work to the best of your ability, then let it go. Instead of seeking absolute perfection in any one project, learn from each one and apply what you learned to the next project you decide to tackle.

26

1. When have you left a project unfinished because it wasn't perfect?

_____

_____

_____

_____

_____

_____

2. What are reasonable, actionable steps you can take to decide whether or not a project is done?

_____

_____

_____

_____

_____

_____

day 9

———— " ————

You may not control all the events that happen to you, but you can decide not to be reduced by them.

Maya Angelou

We can't always predict what will happen in our lives. No matter how carefully we plan, there is an overwhelming amount of actions and events that we don't have control over. We should focus our time and energy on what we know we can control: ourselves.

Unless we're wildly lucky, we cannot go through life without experiencing hardship and heartbreak. Life is beautiful, but it hurts sometimes. When we're challenged, we have a choice: we can grow better or we can grow bitter. It's easy to bemoan your life and circumstances. And it's okay to grieve and mourn for what could have or should have been, but we can decide to stop there or we can decide to grow from the experience. Instead of becoming angry and bitter when life challenges you, challenge it back. Rise up and become stronger and braver than before. You can't control what happens to you, but you can choose to make the most out of whatever life hands you.

1. Are there events in your life that have reduced you to less than you want to be?

_____

_____

_____

_____

_____

_____

_____

2. How can you use challenging events as opportunities for growth?

_____

_____

_____

_____

_____

_____

_____

day 10

The thing that is really hard and really amazing is giving up being perfect and beginning the work of becoming yourself.

Anna Quindlen

No one, not a single one of us, is capable of being perfect. When we spend time trying to be our personal definition of good or perfect, it can be hard to let it go. We all want to be good and to do what's right, but that doesn't have to involve doing anything perfectly. In fact, the most amazing thing we can do is to try to do what's good and what's right enthusiastically, even if imperfectly. Imperfection gives us the opportunity to grow and learn that perfection doesn't. We can't learn to be good or to be right if we don't make mistakes.

When we work on becoming ourselves, we're bound to make mistakes. We're not free from accidentally saying or doing the wrong thing, so embrace it as part of the learning experience. We learn from our mistakes and we can't make mistakes if we're perfect. Releasing yourself from the idea of perfection gives you permission to make mistakes, grow, and come into your best self.

1. Describe a time when you learned and grew from making a mistake.

_____

_____

_____

_____

_____

_____

2. What words or phrases can help you feel more comfortable making mistakes?

_____

_____

_____

_____

_____

_____

days 11-20

---

hu·mil·i·ty

/(h)yoo'milədē/

noun

being perfectly aware that one's true self is no better or worse than others

---

day 11

You can't please everyone, and you can't make everyone like you.

Katie Couric

It's hard to accept that we can't make everyone like us. When we put in genuine efforts to be the best we can be, we expect others to appreciate and approve of us. The uncomfortable truth of the matter is that no matter what we do, some people just won't dole out the admiration we crave.

It's healthy and realistic to accept that there are some people, no matter how kind or generous you are, who simply won't like you. Their not liking you doesn't make you any less valuable to the world than if they did. You, no matter how much or how little of yourself you give to others, are valuable. Your worth doesn't lie within your likability. Don't waste your time and energy trying to please everyone because, at the end of the day, you are valuable no matter how many people like you.

1. Who are you going out of your way to please?

_____

_____

_____

_____

_____

_____

2. What are some qualities that make you valuable?

_____

_____

_____

_____

_____

_____

_____

day 12

————— " —————

When you have expectations, you are setting yourself up for disappointment.

Ryan Reynolds

Everyone has expectations. Even when you're not necessarily aware of them, you have expectations. If you're helping someone, whether you know it or not, you could be expecting something in return. Maybe you'd like them to promise to return the favor or tell you how much they appreciate you. When these expectations aren't met, you are bound to become disappointed, resentful, and maybe even angry. This cycle is difficult to break, but by reframing your time and energy as a gift rather than something you'd like to have paid back, you can move toward humble, open giving without risking resentment.

Think of how good it feels to freely give a gift. It's rewarding to give something to someone knowing that they will enjoy it. Our time and effort can be gifts, too. When we approach others with an open heart, we feel more rewarded. Giving energy as a gift rather than a loan helps your relationship with yourself and others. Practice letting go of your expectations, and when you do choose to give your time or energy, give it as a gift. Choosing to give ourselves without strings attached is a way to avoid disappointment and practice humility.

1. What expectations do you know you have but don't say?

_____

_____

_____

_____

_____

_____

2. How can you practice giving your time and energy freely?

_____

_____

_____

_____

_____

_____

day 13

When you start loving yourself and respecting your time
and energy, things will change. Get to know your worth,
and your value will go up.

Germany Kent

Have you ever given so much of your own time and
energy to someone else that, at the end of the day,
you didn't have enough left over for yourself?
Sometimes we need to give everything we have for
others, but if you find yourself continuously running out
of time and energy to invest in yourself, you may not
know how valuable you are to *you*.

We may feel more valuable when we give our all in the
service of someone else, but what good are we when we
are tired, worn down, and resentful? Setting healthy
boundaries for yourself benefits everyone. Your time
and energy is a finite resource. It runs out and it's
renewed, but you need to use discretion in how you
spend it. You've surely heard the old adage: "you can't
pour from an empty cup." Yes, it applies to all of us!
Saving some of your time and energy for yourself only
gives you more to give. A good night's rest will give you
more energy in the morning. A quiet evening at home to
recharge will put you in a better state of mind the next
day. Invest in yourself and your value (to yourself and
others) will increase.

1. How can you spend more time and energy on yourself?

_____

_____

_____

_____

_____

_____

2. What boundaries can you set to protect your time and energy?

_____

_____

_____

_____

_____

_____

day 14

Love is a beautiful feeling. When you love someone then life becomes beautiful. But in loving someone do not forget to love yourself too!

Avijeet Das

If you are someone who demonstrates your love for others by helping or serving, you are in good company! Many people show love and affection by lending a hand. However, if you are a helper, don't forget that you need self-love too.

Sometimes, we get so caught up in how good it feels to be helpful that we start to neglect ourselves. If you don't set boundaries and learn when to gently and lovingly say "no," you may find yourself forgetting to take care of your own needs. When you've reached this level, it may feel that setting boundaries is harsh, but remember that to give love, you need love. And it all starts with you.

Spend time thinking about what self-love acts make you feel refreshed. It could be exercise, a good book, or a manicure. When it comes to self-love, there's no such thing as too "trivial." It's important that you prioritize the acts that make you feel cared for. Once you've established some self-love routines, protect the time and resources it takes to continue them. Your desire to show love by helping and caring for others is wonderful. Just don't forget that you need love too.

1. What routines or rituals do you maintain that make you feel loved?

_____

_____

_____

_____

_____

_____

2. How can you protect the time and resources to maintain your self-love rituals?

_____

_____

_____

_____

_____

_____

day 15

Help someone, you earn a friend. Help someone too much,
you make an enemy

Erol Ozan

No one wants enemies. And certainly not enemies made over the way you show and demonstrate love and affection! However, it is possible to help too much, and if you do, you run the risk of making an enemy of a friend, or arguably worse, yourself. Yesterday we talked about the boundaries we set to protect our time and resources. Don't forget to understand and honor the boundaries of others too.

Helping a loved one is a gracious and noble act as long as it's done freely and out of genuine care. But make sure to listen to who you are helping. It may make you feel good to be a helper, but be open to the possibility that others may want more independence or space to make mistakes on their own. If you fail to step back, they may grow to resent you. Similarly, if you don't step back when you are running low on time or energy, you could very well make a resentful enemy of yourself or those you feel you have to help. Listen to the people you are helping and to yourself to know when to step back. You and your loved ones will benefit from and appreciate it.

1. How can you practice understanding and respecting other people's boundaries when your instinct is to help?

_____

_____

_____

_____

_____

_____

2. Describe a time when you wanted space and independence to handle a problem on your own.

_____

_____

_____

_____

_____

_____

_____

day 16

Love yourself first and everything else falls into line. You really have to love yourself to get anything done in this world.

Lucille Ball

Lucille Ball was a funny woman, but she took her self-care seriously. Think of the people you most admire: an actor, an activist, or a family member. Do you suppose they could be the powerful, influential force in your life that they are without taking time to care and work on themselves? Sick, exhausted, unwell people can't get their best work done. At their worst, they can't get any work done at all.

Society has made self-love and the act of self-care out to be a selfish, luxurious exercise that should be a reward for hard work rather than a normal part of daily personal maintenance. However, without people "selfishly" taking time out of their busy schedules to care for themselves, our society would crumble into an overwhelmed, exhausted heap! You will be the best version of you when you invest in the love and care that you, just as much as anyone else, need and deserve. When you feel your best, you do you best. Take time to love yourself so you can love you and everyone else the best that you can.

1. How does a lack of self-love and care impact your daily life?

_____

_____

_____

_____

_____

_____

2. What parts of your life improve when you take the time to care for yourself?

_____

_____

_____

_____

_____

_____

day 17

The sad thing that many of us empaths don't realize is that often our desire to heal others is a disguised cry for help for our own healing. Because many of us weren't taught how to value or nurture ourselves at a young age, we tend to unconsciously seek out our own healing in the healing of others.

Mateo Sol

If you find yourself adapting to and absorbing the moods and energies around you, you are an empathetic person. Empathy is a beautiful, powerful trait, but without healthy boundaries, you may find yourself filling holes in your life by helping others instead of helping yourself.

Lending a hand isn't necessarily a cry for help. But carefully examine your motivations the next time you volunteer for a function or offer to help a friend. If you've spent your life devoting your time and attention to others, you might not see your true motivations right away. Chances are, if you are always putting the needs of others before your own, you are trying to carve a space for yourself in their lives as a valuable, worthy individual. It isn't unhealthy to help. But it isn't good for you to help for the sake of healing yourself. Instead of helping to heal yourself, learn to take care of your needs outside of acts of service. You'll become a more fulfilled, more generous, more aware person.

1. How does caring for other people make you feel?

_____

_____

_____

_____

_____

_____

2. How can you validate yourself without turning to others?

_____

_____

_____

_____

_____

_____

_____

"

How good something is should never be determined by its cost, designer, origin, or its perceived value by others.

Ashly Lorenza

When we are sought after for our skills or gifts, we might attach our sense of value to how much we're needed. It feels good to be needed at the bake sale or to help a friend move, but you're valuable even if you don't bake a dozen cookies or load a truck. What you give to others and how they feel about your service is not a reflection of your worth. You are valuable for who you are outside of how much you give to others.

Value is a tricky subject because it's subjective. What one person sees as important may be useless to someone else. The good news is that life, every life, is important no matter what we give or get out of it. Simply by existing, you are valuable. The people who benefit from your goodness would agree that, even if you weren't involved in assisting them, you would still be a valuable person. You are valuable because you are you. Your generosity is just a nice bonus.

1. What is something valuable to you but not to anyone else?

_____

_____

_____

_____

_____

_____

2. Is that item or object good even though it doesn't benefit anyone else?

_____

_____

_____

_____

_____

_____

day 19

The surest way to lose your self-worth is by trying to find it through the eyes of others.

Becca Lee

It isn't a secret that seeking our self-worth through external validation isn't the best way to find it. In fact, our self-worth *can't* come from external sources such as ratings, ranks, or grades because they only measure how we do – not who we are. Others can try to tell you what or how much you're worth, but the only one who can truly determine that is you.

Real accomplishments can and should be taken into account when you're developing your sense of self, but you should also take into consideration the uncountable, intangible qualities that make you who you are. You can ask others what makes you unique and you can use those ideas, but no one else can determine your worth. To work on developing your sense of self-worth, stop measuring how much you do or who you do it for. Learn to differentiate between your role in the lives of others and your own appreciation for your thoughts and feelings. You can find self-worth, but the fastest way to lose it is by trying to find it in others.

1. What are the unique, intangible traits that make you unique?

_____

_____

_____

_____

_____

_____

_____

2. How do you try to measure your self-worth?

_____

_____

_____

_____

_____

_____

_____

day 20

You will be your best self when you take time to understand what you really need, feel, and want.

Deborah Day

If everyone else's needs are satisfied, we might think that, then and only then, we can finally relax and think about ourselves. But there will *always* be people who need something. And you will always find some reason to look out for others before yourself. It's a noble trait, but no one can stay happy and thriving in an environment where they can't fulfill their own needs.

If you've created an environment where you help everyone else before you take care of yourself, it's time to work on rebuilding it. It may seem backwards, but if your own needs aren't met, you are not going to do well when trying to meet anyone else's. If a plane is crashing, you always put your oxygen mask on first. It isn't selfish – it's good sense. You will operate your best when you understand your needs and feelings and can meet them. Instead of rushing to help others, spend some time in reflection. What are your current, most urgent needs? If you're hungry, feed yourself. If you're tired, rest. You won't be your best self if you're always hungry or tired or needing. It might feel selfish at first, but the difference in caring for people after you've cared for yourself is magnificent.

1. What are your current, most urgent needs?

_____

_____

_____

_____

_____

_____

2. What other needs in your life should you take time to meet?

_____

_____

_____

_____

_____

_____

days 21-30

---

au·then·tic·i·ty

/ˌôTHenˈtisədē/

noun

representing one's true nature or beliefs; true to oneself or to the person identified

---

day 21

Learning to let go is not giving up! It is simply passing the burden to a better fighter, so you can fight another day.

Shannon L. Alder

Perfectionism holds us captive to our own impossibly high standards and unending to-do lists. Perfectionism is a display for others and not progress for us. To release ourselves, we should learn to let go of our expectations and our desire to work until everything is "perfect."

Letting go of our self-imposed burdens isn't easy. It's a daily challenge that asks us to choose between how we appear to others and how we feel about ourselves. How often have you felt overwhelmed and resentful of the image you are trying to keep up? Letting go of the image you're trying to present will give you back the time and energy you're pouring into it. What good could you do for yourself with that time and energy? It isn't easy and it doesn't happen immediately, but allowing yourself to let go will give you the space to grow and develop your character so that the person you present to others is the truest, happiest version of yourself.

1. What on your to-do list can you let go?

_____

_____

_____

_____

_____

_____

2. How can you prioritize your self-development over your image?

_____

_____

_____

_____

_____

_____

day 22

You wouldn't worry so much about what others think of you
if you realized how seldom they do.

Eleanor Roosevelt

How often do you judge other people? When you judge others, how much time and energy do you spend thinking about them? More often than not, you likely only spend a few seconds formulating an opinion, forget that opinion moments later, and then go about the rest of your day.

It's human nature to worry about what others think of us. It's good to be aware of others and to be polite and considerate. But if you don't spend much time deciding what you think of others, it stands to reason that others don't spend their energy thinking about you either. Isn't that liberating? We don't need to devote all of our time and energy to creating a persona to show to the rest of the world. We can be free to be our true, authentic selves without worrying about what others think – because they probably aren't thinking very much at all!

If you've spent a lot of time developing a persona, it could be hard to begin practicing authenticity, but be assured: no one cares about the image you present to the world more than you do. Identify the parts of yourselves that you present to others that aren't really "you" and practice removing them from your life.

1. What do you do on a daily basis to maintain an image?

_____

_____

_____

_____

_____

_____

_____

2. Which parts of your image are for the benefit of others and not yourself?

_____

_____

_____

_____

_____

_____

_____

day 23

Every twist and turn in life is an opportunity to learn something new about yourself, your interests, your talents, and how to set them and achieve goals.

Jameela Jamil

No matter how hard we try or how badly we want something, we are bound to experience failure or interruptions at some point. It's inevitable – but we can choose to let setbacks define us, or we can take our failures and interruptions and reinterpret them as unique, positive opportunities to learn about ourselves.

Failure and setbacks can feel even worse when we are trying to meet the expectations of others as well as our own. When you are a high-achieving person, setbacks can shake your sense of self. Remember that everyone experiences setbacks. Instead of allowing them to define you, refocus on what you can learn. The next time something doesn't work out for you, think of how your talents could be better used, your desires better realized, and how you can use the knowledge you gained to move forward.

1. Describe a time when you experienced a setback in a goal you were working toward. How did you respond?

_____

_____

_____

_____

_____

_____

_____

2. How did that setback help you learn about your talents, desires, and the goals you want to achieve?

_____

_____

_____

_____

_____

_____

_____

day 24

If you spent your life concentrating on what everyone else thought of you, would you forget who you really were?

Jodi Picoult

Yesterday we talked about how infrequently people truly think about us and how we develop personas. To a certain extent, we all develop personas. We're different people at work than we are at home, for example. It's okay to adjust your behavior based on your environment, but when you're not even sure who the "real" you is when you go home, you might be forgetting who you really are.

If you've spent your life trying to live up to expectations of others and chasing down your goals, you might not realize that you're unsure of what you want or that you've forgotten who you truly are. The realization can be unsettling; especially if you've started to over-identify with your persona instead of your authentic self. Instead of panicking, practice re-discovering yourself. Start journaling and noticing patterns about what brings you joy and what brings you stress. Focus on what you genuinely enjoy and you'll start becoming the most authentic version of yourself. Begin acknowledging the expectations of others rather than absorbing them. As you parse external expectations from internal desires, you'll begin recognizing yourself.

1. What would bring you immense joy even if no one else knew about it?

_____

_____

_____

_____

_____

_____

_____

2. What are some hobbies and pastimes you've neglected while pursuing your goals?

_____

_____

_____

_____

_____

_____

_____

day 25

I'm learning how to drown out the constant noise that is such an inseparable part of my life. I don't have to prove anything to anyone. I only have to follow my heart and concentrate on what I want to say to the world. I run my world.

Beyoncé

The world around us is full of noise. There are commercials selling us products to be better in one way or another, companies and corporations pushing us to work harder, and even well-meaning friends and family encouraging us to reach our fullest potential. With the constant noise from the outside having such a powerful influence on our lives, how can we even hope to practice following our own paths?

The journey toward authenticity begins with recognizing outside influences. Think about the work you do or the products you buy. Who or what drove those decisions? Think also about your behavior or your appearance. We each have control of these decisions and we can choose to be influenced or not. It's okay to make decisions to fit financial situations or fashion trends, but once you identify your influences, you can begin choosing whether or not to continue listening. When you can decide whether or not to follow outside influences, then you can truly begin running your own world as your authentic self.

1. What are some obvious influences in your life?

_____

_____

_____

_____

_____

_____

_____

2. Who or what is influencing you in a way that you like? Don't like?

_____

_____

_____

_____

_____

_____

_____

_____ " _____

I have learned that as long as I hold fast to my beliefs and values – and follow my own moral compass – then the only expectations I need to live up to are my own.
Michelle Obama

You know yourself better than anyone else. You have the unique ability to decide what your beliefs and values are. Others can share theirs or even push theirs on you, but only you can decide what you believe in. If you've lived your life striving to live up to the expectations of others, deciding what you believe in can be a daunting task. The expectations and beliefs we take from others can be a way to measure our success and a way to set goals. But, when you're striking out to live up to your own beliefs and expectations, you may not know where to start.

Breaking free of the expectations of others is more than choosing to set your own goals and expectations, it's a challenge to decide what's best for you. When someone is influencing your choices and decisions, it may feel safe. You are relying on someone else to decide what you look like or how you behave or what you believe. But you are also counting on other people for praise and recognition. Relying on yourself and your own sense of what's right and wrong gives you the freedom to act and think as you please and releases you from the pressure of outside validation.

1. List some of your closely-held beliefs and values.

_____

_____

_____

_____

_____

_____

_____

2. Which of those beliefs and values have you developed for yourself and which have you taken on from others?

_____

_____

_____

_____

_____

_____

_____

day 27

The need to prove who you are will vanish once you know
who you are.

Danielle Pierre

If you are competitive, the need to come out on top is hard-wired into your mind. For some people, being competitive manifests as a need to level-up based on an internal metric. Others feel a need to prove something to others. Where do you fall on this spectrum?

It could be uncomfortable to consider that you've been working so hard to achieve goals that weren't even for yourself, but recognizing it is the only way out. To figure out who you might be trying to prove yourself to, ask yourself a few questions. When you've completed a project or reached a goal, who do you most want to see it? Who do you want to hear tell you that you've done a good job? Of course, it's nice to be congratulated, but if you find yourself constantly craving praise, you could be working to prove yourself to someone else.

We may need some time and space to determine who we are and what we truly want and care about. But, when we do, the drive to prove ourselves to other people will go away. We can begin to experience the empowerment of working toward our own goals and ambitions to demonstrate our hard work to ourselves.

1. Who do you most want to be congratulated by? Why do you think that is?

_____

_____

_____

_____

_____

_____

_____

2. Describe a time when you went above and beyond to prove yourself to someone else.

_____

_____

_____

_____

_____

_____

_____

day 28

If you care about what people think about you, you will end up being their slave. Reject and pull your own rope.

Auliq Ice

It's in our nature to care what others think of us. However, you don't need to allow other people's opinions to control you. If you struggle with this, you may find yourself adjusting to fit what you think others would like the most. When you care too much about the thoughts and opinions of others, you inevitably edit and censor your true self to try to fit into each person's ideal mold. You stop being your own person and become a shapeshifter who morphs into whatever others want of you.

Instead, practice "pulling your own rope," when you find yourself adjusting based off the thoughts and opinions of others, challenge yourself to think of how your true self would act or speak. When you practice authenticity, keep in mind that you may confuse and upset some people if your true self doesn't match the mask you've been presenting. It's hard work, but it's much harder to keep morphing into different molds that aren't even the real you. You may never stop caring what others think of you, but you can stop letting their opinions control you.

1. What are you afraid of others thinking about you?

_____

_____

_____

_____

_____

_____

2. How do you censor your true self in daily life?

_____

_____

_____

_____

_____

_____

day 29

Personal empowerment is about knowing your answers come from inside. While you may need validation when you are unsure, you will not need approval. Approval seeking will forever keep you underpowered.

Daphne Michaels

The difference between validation and approval is subtle. It lies in what you are looking for. If you seek validation, you are looking for reassurance that you are on the right path or moving in a positive direction. When you seek approval, you are looking for permission to continue on a certain trajectory. By seeking approval instead of validation, you risk limiting yourself to the ideas and expectations of others.

Personal empowerment means that you trust your own direction and make your own decisions because you are confident in who you are and what you are doing. You may need guidance along the way, but, if you are true to yourself, you will not need anyone's permission. Today, practice noticing the difference between validation and approval. Notice when you are looking for one or the other and why. We all need guidance from time to time, but none of us need permission to be true to ourselves.

1. What does validation look like to you? How do you want to be validated?

_____

_____

_____

_____

_____

_____

_____

2. Who do you look to when you want approval? Why?

_____

_____

_____

_____

_____

_____

_____

day 30

I define me. You don't.

Miya Yamanouchi

It can take an entire lifetime to confidently define yourself, determine what you stand for, and decide who you want to be. But the power to make those important decisions lies only within yourself. You, and no one else, have the power to define your true self. It could be easier, in some ways, to allow others to dictate your career path or political views. Going with the flow can bring superficial peace to your life and relationships, but it won't bring you authenticity.

You have the power to define yourself based on your own thoughts and desires. Consider the influences in your life and evaluate their role and how much weight they carry. Then, craft a mission statement to describe how you want to live out what you believe. A mission statement will empower you to define yourself and your behavior. When you take up the responsibility to be authentically you, you take on the responsibility to decide what defines you. It's a significant task, but a significant freedom. Give yourself the space to learn what defines you and then act on it. The power is all yours.

1. Write a mission statement: what do you stand for?

_____

_____

_____

_____

_____

_____

_____

2. How can you carry out your mission statement every day?

_____

_____

_____

_____

_____

_____

_____

---

e·qua·nim·i·ty

/ˌekwəˈnimədē/

noun

mental calmness, composure, and evenness of temper, especially in a difficult situation

---

_____ " _____

Feelings are just visitors, let them come and go.

Mooji

Many of us are familiar with powerful, sometimes overwhelming feelings. Some of us are also familiar with being completely consumed with emotions in a way that affects our moods in big, long-term ways. For those of us who find ourselves consumed with our feelings, those feelings can make or break an entire day. Feelings are important parts of our lives, but it's equally important to put boundaries in place so feelings don't rule our lives.

Rather than allowing your emotions to take up more room than they deserve, allow yourself to feel them and then let them go. Acknowledge your feelings but don't force them to stick around or allow yourself to be consumed by them. It's tempting to hang onto emotions we like or harbor unpleasant ones to set a mood, but holding onto a feeling isn't sustainable. Go ahead and enjoy the wonder of a beautiful sunset or the nostalgia of old photographs. Then, allow those feelings to dissipate naturally. By letting emotions come and go, you're allowing yourself to live in the moment and open yourself up to the constant ebb and flow of feelings. Feelings are great. Make sure to give them all the time and space they deserve.

1. What emotions do you find yourself holding onto?

_____

_____

_____

_____

_____

_____

2. What actions can you take to make sure you're giving your feelings space to come and go?

_____

_____

_____

_____

_____

_____

_____

day 32

Without leaps of imagination or dreaming, we lose the
excitement of possibilities. Dreaming, after all, is a form of
planning.

Gloria Steinem

Dreamers and those of us who enjoy imagining possibilities may find ourselves feeling stifled by a society that wants us to be realistic and to have concrete plans. If we are at odds with the idea of who we need to be to get by life and who we feel we truly are, we might struggle to feel at home anywhere.

Sometimes the message from outside may be to choose reality over dreams, but you don't have to give up one or the other. Instead of trying to be someone you aren't, allow yourself to dream and imagine. Dreamers and creative individuals need space to explore the unrealistic and it's okay to fuel that fire. Go ahead and dream and imagine all of the possibilities your life could be because, even if it seems lofty or idealistic, when you experience strong emotions, you often also have a powerful ability to think and dream in unique ways. Allow yourself the space to think and dream because, when we dream, we get excited about our lives and the endless possibilities.

1. What are some of your dreams for your life?

_____

_____

_____

_____

_____

_____

2. How can you allow yourself more space to dream
and imagine?

_____

_____

_____

_____

_____

_____

day 33

Only you can take inner freedom away from yourself, or give it to yourself. Nobody else can.

Michael A. Singer

If you feel trapped in a society, job, or family that doesn't understand you, you are not alone. Creative, emotional people often feel like the odd one out at work or events and even within friend and family groups. If you feel misunderstood or unappreciated for your unique qualities, you may feel tempted to act differently around people. You may go so far as to censor or edit yourself to better fit in. However, that decision lies only within you.

It might feel like the people around you want a toned down, edited version of yourself, but that isn't a decision they can make. You alone hold the power to be or not to be yourself. Don't fall into the trap of thinking that others are forcing you to be one way or another because you are the only one who can decide if you have the freedom to be yourself or not. Today, work on noticing when you feel the need to modify your thoughts or behavior to fit into a group. Consider who you modify your behavior for and why you do it. Then, make the conscious decision to be yourself. You have inner freedom and only you can take it away. Go ahead and be your free, true self.

1. How do you find yourself modifying your behavior to fit in?

_____

_____

_____

_____

_____

_____

_____

2. How can you give freedom back to yourself?

_____

_____

_____

_____

_____

_____

_____

day 34

How would your life be different if…You stopped validating your victim mentality? Let today be the day…You shake off your self-defeating drama and embrace your innate ability to recover and achieve.

Steve Maraboli

It's too easy to feel like the victim. Especially when you feel that you can't be yourself in a world that doesn't understand your uniqueness. However, victim mentality suppresses your true powers of strength and resilience. Instead of allowing yourself to feel like there isn't a place for you, you can use your natural strengths and talents to make a place for yourself.

When you experience strong emotions, you may be more likely to fall into a victim mentality, but you are also uniquely gifted in handling strong feelings. Instead of embracing the victim mentality, we can choose to rise up and embrace our natural resilience. Self-defeating, victim mentality gets in the way of our growth and development while resilience develops our empathy and wisdom. It isn't fun to experience hardship, but there's a wealth of growth that can come from it as long as we choose to recover rather than recede.

1. In what ways are you accepting a victim mentality in your life?

_____

_____

_____

_____

_____

_____

_____

2. How can you practice resilience?

_____

_____

_____

_____

_____

_____

_____

day 35

The first place where self-esteem begins its journey is within us.

Stephen Richards

Most of us have experienced low self-esteem at one time or another. We live in a competitive world with media that bombards us with exceptionally talented and intelligent people. We can try to build our self-esteem by turning to our friends and family for encouragement, but we can't build healthy self-esteem without developing it within ourselves first.

Self-esteem is a concept that balances on our own thoughts. If we think nicely about ourselves, we are more likely to have healthy self-esteem. But, if we experience a lot of negative thoughts, we are more likely to have low, unhealthy self-esteem.

Since our self-esteem comes from what we think of ourselves, we must start there. Challenge negative, self-deprecating thoughts or thoughts that compare you to anyone else. Once you feel more secure within yourself, your performance anxieties and fear of failure will diminish. It's a cycle: if you speak kindly to yourself, you will have less fear of failure, and less of a tendency to speak badly of yourself when you fall short of your goals, leading to healthy self-esteem. We can all stand to benefit from positive self-talk and higher, healthier self-esteem.

1. What are three things that you like about yourself?

_____

_____

_____

_____

_____

_____

2. What is a negative thing you frequently say about yourself? How can you challenge that thought with a positive one?

_____

_____

_____

_____

_____

_____

day 36

Every spoken sentence beginning with 'I Am' is a powerful spell exhaled into action. Describe yourself wisely.

Dacha Avelin

Self-deprecation is a common comedy technique, but it can have a devastating effect on self-esteem. You may get a laugh from friends when you bemoan a trait you dislike about yourself, but what does it do to you? Not only can self-deprecation have a negative impact on your self-esteem, but you may also create self-fulfilling prophecies for your behavior. You are much more likely to become what you say you are, so make sure you are always describing yourself in the positive light you want to see.

For example, saying "I am disorganized" isn't likely to make you feel better about that trait and it certainly isn't likely to turn you into an organized person. However, describing yourself with positive words has a positive effect on your self-esteem and acts as a personal call to action. "I am brave," or "I am kind" are two personal, powerful mantras. We are what we say we are. Take great care in the way you describe yourself so that you, and those around you, believe those positive words. Describe yourself positively because, as we all know, words have immense power.

1. What words will you use to positively describe yourself?

_____

_____

_____

_____

_____

_____

2. How can you remind yourself of your positive traits every day?

_____

_____

_____

_____

_____

_____

day 37

Authentic happiness is not linked to an activity; it is a state of being, a profound emotional balance struck by a subtle understanding of how the mind functions.

Mattieu Ricard

It's an easy mistake to make: participating in an activity that makes us happy seems like it makes us happy people. Unfortunately, happiness isn't so simple. For those of us who experience strong and, at times, volatile emotions, the coming and going of happiness can be a source of stress. Instead of trying to chase the activities that make us happy, we should work on creating lasting, sustainable happiness within ourselves.

Emotional balance isn't naturally easy for everyone to achieve, but we all start at the same place: understanding how our emotions work. Feelings may be prompted by activities, words or people, but they are generated in our own minds. Therefore, happiness comes from ourselves, and not the people or activities that make us happy. If we count on others and the world around us to make us happy, we give up control and responsibility of our feelings, and put ourselves at risk for profound hurt and disappointment. Instead, creating and cultivating our happiness from inside will bring us a more secure, long-lasting happiness that no one can take away.

1. What activities make you feel happy?

_____

_____

_____

_____

_____

_____

_____

2. How can you create contentment in your daily life?

_____

_____

_____

_____

_____

_____

_____

day 38

Anyone can be angry—that is easy. But to be angry with
the right person, to the right degree, at the right time, for
the right purpose, and in the right way—that is not easy

Aristotle

Has your anger ever gotten in the way of your daily routine? If yes, you're human. As Aristotle says, being angry is easy. For those of us with strong feelings, our anger can sometimes take over and bleed into other, unrelated parts of our lives. When that happens, it stops being constructive or purposeful, and becomes an unpleasant, distracting feeling.

It's okay to be angry, but it's also okay to let your anger go. Instead of hanging onto anger and turning it into a closely held grudge, evaluate the situation and decide if it's helpful to stay angry. In many cases, it probably isn't. Think of the ripple effect your anger can have –if you're angry with a coworker and snap at your local barista, who then takes it out on her friend, your anger has travelled much farther and unnecessarily for no reason! It can be difficult to let go of anger when it's appropriate, but doing so will ultimately help us become more peaceful, balanced people.

1. Is there a grudge or something you're angry about that you can let go of?

_____

_____

_____

_____

_____

_____

_____

2. What are some ways you can release anger in the moment before starting a new task or conversation?

_____

_____

_____

_____

_____

_____

_____

day 39

To increase your effectiveness, make your emotions
subordinate to your commitments.

Brian Koslow

How often do you put off a commitment or a task because you didn't "feel like it?" Many people don't necessarily feel like paying bills or doing the dishes, but imagine if no one ever actually fulfilled his or her responsibilities! Emotions can easily get in the way of our obligations if we let them. Let's practice putting our commitments over our emotions so we can become more effective in our personal, work, or academic lives.

It's selfish to put your feelings above a given responsibility. If you do it often enough, you risk being perceived as lazy or unreliable, even if that isn't true. To work on making your feelings subordinate, work on balancing how you feel with how you behave. Allow yourself to be presented as calm and collected, even if you're feeling the opposite. Encourage yourself to begin and complete tasks, even if they aren't as poignant as you'd like. With time, effort, and practice, you'll be able to set your feelings aside to reliably carry out your responsibilities.

1. Which tasks do you put off until you're in the right mood?

_____

_____

_____

_____

_____

_____

2. What can you physically do to ensure you complete tasks and responsibilities despite your feelings?

_____

_____

_____

_____

_____

_____

—————"—————

Remember that failure is an event, not a person.

Zig Ziglar

Sometimes, when we've worked hard and put our heart and soul into a project or toward a goal, we take it personally when we fail. Failure is a painful and unfortunately unavoidable part of life. However, we can build a healthy relationship with failure if we can see it as an event instead of a reflection of ourselves and our abilities.

Failure happens to everyone. But failure happens *to* you, not *because of* you. If we choose to define ourselves by our failures rather than what we learned from them, no one would ever advance. It's okay to feel the negative feelings that come from failure. It's natural to feel disappointment, but you personally aren't a disappointment. Your feelings do not define you any more than your failures do. When we become balanced between our behavior and our feelings, we can allow failure to happen, and let it go like any other emotion. Emotional balance is about accepting feelings as they come and then letting them go when they stop being productive. Don't hang onto negative feelings or events such as failure, and allow them to get in the way of the rest of your life.

1. Describe a time when you took a failure personally.
How did it affect you?

_____

_____

_____

_____

_____

_____

2. How can you work to see failure more objectively?

_____

_____

_____

_____

_____

_____

non·at·tach·ment

/nän əˈtaCHmənt/

noun

moving through life without letting things, people, or places have a hold on you

Days 41-50 • Enneagram 5 • Nonattachment

day 41

I always did something I was a little not ready to do. I think that's how you grow. When there's that moment of 'Wow, I'm not really sure I can do this,' and you push through those moments, that's when you have a breakthrough.

Marissa Mayer

For those of us who prefer to be fully prepared for everything, trying something we're not ready to do is asking a lot. It's easier to stay within our comfort zones and wait to act until we have all of the facts or know all the information. However, when we push ourselves, we can begin to grow in ways we never expected.

Trying something new can be uncomfortable. It's common to have fears that you won't be able to carry out a new task or activity, or that you'll look silly doing it. That may be true, but you'll also learn something. When you begin pushing yourself, you can push further and further until you have "breakthroughs," and open the doors to new, exciting activities. Start with the smallest tasks or activities you haven't yet felt ready to do. Taking small steps outside of your comfort zone will increase your daring and confidence until you can push yourself through the moments of fear and uncertainty. Start small, and soon you'll be seeing big results.

1. What is one task or activity you've been avoiding because you didn't feel prepared?

_____

_____

_____

_____

_____

_____

_____

2. What worries you the most about trying something you don't feel ready for?

_____

_____

_____

_____

_____

_____

_____

day 42

Your attitude, not your aptitude, will determine your altitude.

Zig Zagler

You've seen the posters around the gym or in the library that say "hard work beats talent when talent doesn't work hard." There are several ways of saying that attitude goes further than aptitude, and it's the truth. When we want to be competent, we need to rely on our mindset just as much as our skills. It's important to acknowledge that it is our attitude just as much as our ability that affects our competency.

The next time you're worrying about whether or not you're competent enough for a task, check your attitude. If you are fearful or anxious, you're unlikely to perform well. However, if you approach the task with confidence and serenity, you're more likely to keep a level head and do well. Our attitudes have more influence on us than we tend to give them credit for. If you want to feel confident and competent, approach your tasks and problems with a calm, capable attitude. Knowledge and skill are only small pieces of the puzzle that make up whether or not we are successful. Make sure your attitude is positive and open. Everything else will fall in line if your mindset is correct.

1. Describe your attitude when it comes to new or difficult tasks.

_____

_____

_____

_____

_____

_____

2. What are some words or mantras you can develop to improve your attitude?

_____

_____

_____

_____

_____

_____

day 43

Our feelings are not there to be cast out or conquered.
They're there to be engaged and expressed with
imagination and intelligence.

T.K. Coleman

Those of us who prefer not to engage with our feelings might see them as something to be ignored or overcome. This may come from our desire to feel objective and in-control or from a desire to maintain a rational image. Feelings aren't necessarily rational and they aren't always efficient, but that doesn't mean they aren't valuable.

Feelings can make us feel out of control or that we don't know what is happening inside of us. This is the source of a lot of fear and discomfort. However, humans are skilled in reason and thought. There's no reason why we shouldn't be able to acknowledge our feelings and express them while maintaining our rational minds. Feelings tell us a lot about our state of mind and our surroundings. It's one of the many ways to observe and experience the world around us. Instead of sweeping emotions under the rug, allow yourself to engage with them. Label them, name them, and allow yourself to think about them. Emotions are one part of our lives and they are just as worth examining as anything else.

1. Which feelings do you try to suppress or ignore?

_____

_____

_____

_____

_____

_____

_____

2. In which ways can you engage with your feelings more often?

_____

_____

_____

_____

_____

_____

_____

day 44

One way to boost our willpower and focus is to manage our distractions instead of letting them manage us.

Daniel Goleman

Do you have personal projects or hobbies that take up a lot of your free time? Many people have personal projects that act more as a distraction from everyday life than a true hobby. Rather than allowing yourself to escape from reality or responsibility, practice managing your distractions so you can continue to be a competent, focused individual.

If your hobby has become more of a distraction than a genuine interest, define boundaries around it to stop you from spending too much time on it. Set time limits or schedule specific times to work on your projects. When you can define the time you'll spend on it, you can focus on your more pressing needs and responsibilities. When we're stressed or overwhelmed, we are prone to fall into our pet projects and interests and ignore life around us. Instead, we should aim to be more present in daily life and resist the urge to escape reality through distractions.

1. Which hobbies do you use as a distraction from daily life?

_____

_____

_____

_____

_____

_____

_____

2. How can you designate time to work on your hobbies while maintaining focus on daily tasks and goals?

_____

_____

_____

_____

_____

_____

_____

day 45

Just try new things. Don't be afraid. Step out of your
comfort zone and soar, all right?

Michelle Obama

It's easier said than done, isn't it? Trying new things forces us to be vulnerable. When we try new things, we have to admit that we're unsure and unfamiliar and it's uncomfortable. But when we really think about it, what is there to lose from taking the risk of trying something different? It's nice to be an expert, but we have nothing to learn if we always choose activities or tasks that we're familiar with. Instead of limiting ourselves only to what we know, we should take chances and explore what we don't know.

When we push the boundaries of our own comfort zone, we'll feel resistance. We prefer to be comfortable and stick to what we know. But when we step outside of our comfort zones and make a regular habit of it, our comfort zone will grow with us. And, when we're growing at that rate, nothing can stop us. The real question isn't "what do we have to lose" from taking a risk, it's "what do we have to gain?"

1. Which new tasks, responsibilities, or ideas are you hesitant to explore because they're unfamiliar?

_____

_____

_____

_____

_____

_____

_____

2. How do you think you stand to grow it you choose to be vulnerable and take on the new challenges?

_____

_____

_____

_____

_____

_____

_____

"

If you're making mistakes, then you are making new things, trying new things, learning, living, pushing yourself, changing your world. You're doing things you've never done before and more importantly, you're doing something.

Neil Gaiman

Mistakes are an unavoidable part of growth and development. If we're not making mistakes, chances are that we also aren't growing. Learning is an inherently vulnerable process, and we're bound to experience shortcomings and mistakes along the way. Mistakes aren't failures – they're lessons. When we're just starting out on undertaking a new challenge, we can't expect ourselves to do it perfectly. It takes time and patience to develop the skills to do something well. Mistakes mean that we're pushing our boundaries and learning.

The most important part of trying something new isn't necessarily the task or responsibility itself. The important thing is that you've accepted the challenge and have the intention of learning and putting yourself in a vulnerable position. From a personal development standpoint, the fact that you took action at all is more important than the action you took! We're all going to make mistakes when we take new actions, but our mistakes will be our lessons as we continue to tackle new horizons and change our worlds.

1. What mistakes are you afraid of making?

_____

_____

_____

_____

_____

_____

_____

2. What do you stand to learn from making those mistakes?

_____

_____

_____

_____

_____

_____

_____

day 47

Life is not a spectator sport.

Jackie Robinson

Too easily we can get caught up observing rather than participating. Observing is safe: we can see what's going on without being too near. We can be present without being involved. We often get close enough to see the action, but not so close that we have to be a part of it. Observation removes us from the risk and responsibility of being involved.

Observation is fine when you're about to start a new project or take on a new task, but eventually we have to leave our observation vantage point and get our feet wet. We can't truly learn about love and about life from observation – we really have to get in there and try it for ourselves. We miss out on the nuances and poignancy of life if we just watch it go by. Instead of standing on the sidelines watching life happen to everyone else, start participating. Get involved with something new, introduce yourself, and take small steps toward living your life. You only get one. Don't spend the whole time just watching.

1. Describe a time when you found yourself observing rather than participating.

_____

_____

_____

_____

_____

_____

_____

2. Choose a part of your life to become more involved in. How will you start participating more actively?

_____

_____

_____

_____

_____

_____

_____

———— " ————

The best and most beautiful things in the world cannot be seen or even touched. They must be felt with the heart.

Hellen Keller

We like to be able to look at or hear something and to be able to describe it. It's human nature to want to describe, name, and label things. It helps us see and understand the world around us. To a certain degree, we can describe and name our emotions and feelings. There are some, however, that are too intricate and complex to simply describe. Often these feelings are the deepest and most powerful in the world.

Sometimes we need to let go of our need to describe and label, and learn to enjoy the indescribable parts of our lives. If we spend our time trying to take inventory of our feelings, we're going to miss out on some of the most profound experiences we can encounter. To practice being present with your emotions, step back from your desire to explain or label. Listen to music or look at a painting and notice it for its beauty rather than its technique. Enjoy a sunrise or a good meal without analyzing it. There are many wonderful, observable parts of our lives, but don't miss out on the indescribable.

1. How can you make your feelings more present?

_____

_____

_____

_____

_____

_____

_____

2. What are some ways that you can enjoy beautiful, incredible experiences more fully?

_____

_____

_____

_____

_____

_____

_____

———— " ————

Choose a challenge instead of a competence.

Eleanor Roosevelt

It feels comfortable and secure to do what we already know how to do. If we only take on tasks that we know we're good at, there's little room for error or confusion. But while sticking to what we know ensures that we will know how to do it right, it also ensures that we're not going to grow at another task. Competency feels good because it feels secure, but it's not often that we can grow when we are comfortable and competent.

Instead of choosing to engage in activities you're already competent in, set a goal to challenge yourself. It can be uncomfortable to try new things because we risk looking silly or stupid, but growth isn't always glamorous. Oftentimes, it's rough and awkward. But when we choose to challenge ourselves, we're guaranteed to see growth. When you take on something new, you're temporarily letting go of your competency. But, in time, you'll be proficient at the new activity and be ready to try something new. Competency doesn't stop with one thing. How many tasks can you gain competency in?

1. What's a task you always do because you feel comfortable doing it?

_____

_____

_____

_____

_____

_____

_____

2. Is there a task you're afraid of trying because you don't yet know how to do it? What is it? How can you learn how to do it?

_____

_____

_____

_____

_____

_____

_____

day 50

No one has ever become poor by giving.

Anne Frank

It's human nature to want to hang onto what we feel is scarce. That includes physical goods such as shelter and money, and intangibles such as our emotional energy. However, like Anne Frank says, there's more to be gained by giving than there is by hoarding. Even if we don't have much to give, we won't become poor by sharing it. This includes our time and energy.

Our emotional energy is a renewable source. We might feel emotionally drained or burned out after work or after a long day of socializing, but we will always have some left over for ourselves. Instead of locking ourselves away in our rooms or putting on headphones to drown out the rest of the world, we should work on being more open to it. There are people in your life who want to see and hear from you more than they are right now. If you're afraid that you've already given too much of your energy out today, test your limit. Put down your phone or pause your podcast to spend time with the people who love you. You don't have to conserve your emotional energy, because you'll have more the next day. You'll never become poor by giving more of yourself to your loved ones.

1. What do you do to try and conserve your emotional energy?

_____

_____

_____

_____

_____

_____

2. How can you give more of your time and energy to your loved ones?

_____

_____

_____

_____

_____

_____

_____

cour·age

/ˈkərij/

noun

the ability to act in a way that is not motivated by fear or anxiety

Days 51-60 • Enneagram 6 • Courage

day 51

Anxiety's like a rocking chair. It gives you something to do,
but it doesn't get you very far.

Jodi Picoult

Worry can take up a lot of our time if we allow it to. However, no matter how much we worry, it seldom changes a situation. We can break the cycle of anxious thought patterns and choose to work on becoming courageous and active. Instead of giving our time and energy to anxiety, let's focus on courageous actions, and engaging in positive, focused thoughts.

Worries and nervousness are a healthy and normal part of life, but they can take over our thoughts and actions if we don't learn to redirect ourselves. Anxiety can feel productive if you're imagining how to handle a worst-case-scenario or planning a conversation that may or may not happen, but the reality is that anxious thoughts don't usually lead to action. To release ourselves from fear and develop more courage, we can remind ourselves that worry doesn't necessarily mean action. Instead, we can take courageous actions, such as choosing to engage in focused activities instead of ruminating or changing our thought patterns when we find ourselves worrying.

1. When has worrying about an event changed the outcome?

_____

_____

_____

_____

_____

_____

_____

2. What are some positive, courageous thoughts or mantras you can remind yourself of when you begin to worry?

_____

_____

_____

_____

_____

_____

_____

day 52

Worry often gives a small thing a big shadow.

Swedish Proverb

You've almost certainly heard the phrase "don't make a mountain out of a molehill." Worry must be a universal human experience because there's a similar proverb from every corner of the world! The consensus across all races, languages, and creeds seems to be that worry does nothing more than turn minor fears into major anxieties.

The next time you find yourself worrying, think about how much bigger the problem is becoming in your head. Turning it over and over in your head is likely to cause it to get bigger than it really is and cause you undue stress and anxiety. Worry doesn't make problems go away. It can, however, create more problems for ourselves such as anxiety, insomnia, moodiness, and can even manifest itself in physical symptoms. Instead of fretting, try to put your worries into perspective – how much will what you're fearing matter tomorrow? In a week? A year? Everything, including worries and the events that cause them, will pass. Don't let worry make your fears any bigger or take up more space than they deserve.

1. Describe a time when something you worried about turned out to be much more minor than you had feared.

_____

_____

_____

_____

_____

_____

_____

2. How can you redirect your thoughts so your worries don't grow bigger?

_____

_____

_____

_____

_____

_____

_____

day 53

Fearlessness is like a muscle. I know from my own life that the more I exercise it the more natural it becomes to not let my fears run me.

Arianna Huffington

We don't come across fearlessness naturally. To be fearless, we need to practice being vulnerable and to come out of the experience stronger. In order to become more courageous and to break the cycle of allowing our fears to run us, we must practice bravery by going out and experiencing fear, and learning what it takes to overcome it.

Like anything else in life, certain skills and behaviors require practice. Think of the events or situations that cause you to worry, and imagine how you could practice courageousness for those situations. Maybe you simply need to be more prepared for a task to take it on courageously. Or perhaps role-playing a situation with a friend, or journaling about what you're afraid of and why, could help you practice fearlessness. When the time comes for you to confront what scares you, you'll be more focused and capable. Eventually, after practicing your bravery and by carrying it out over and over again, you'll build your fearlessness muscle and be ready to flex.

1. In which ways do you like to prepare to face your fears?

_____

_____

_____

_____

_____

_____

_____

2. How can you make challenging yourself and practicing fearlessness a regular event?

_____

_____

_____

_____

_____

_____

_____

day 54

_____ ” _____

Life expands or shrinks in proportion to one's courage.

Anais Nin

We have the power to change how big or small our worlds and perspectives are. We can live in the smallest, most sheltered world if we choose. Or, if we have courage, we can open our hearts and minds to the vast, changing world outside our doors. We can choose. But of course, we have to build courage to expand our worldviews. Our worlds are only as big or as small as we make them.

If we're courageous, nothing in the world is off-limits. We can experience anything we seek if we aren't too afraid. We can challenge our worldviews and ideas, test our physical limits, and change our perspectives if we have the courage to do so. Expanding our life is scary. It requires sacrifice, risk, and the potential for failure. But we have the whole world to gain if we put our fears aside and take a chance. To build the courage to expand your life, focus on what you have to gain instead of what you might lose. Think of the possibilities rather than the risks. Don't be reckless, but don't be afraid. There's a whole world that's yours to see, if you want to.

1. In which ways do you want to expand your world?

_____

_____

_____

_____

_____

_____

2. What are some steps you can take to make it happen?

_____

_____

_____

_____

_____

_____

_____

—————— **"** ——————

You cannot swim for new horizons until you have courage
to lose sight of the shore.

William Faulkner

Fear limits us to only what we're comfortable and familiar with. The less we're comfortable with and the more we fear, the smaller and more frightening our worlds become. To expand our comfort zones and our worldviews, we have to engage with our worries and practice courage in the face of fear. Losing sight of our proverbial shores means different things for different people, depending on what your goals and aspirations are.

Stepping outside of our comfort zones requires endurance and bravery. But exploring new horizons doesn't have to be an earth-shattering event. We can start small, with things like trying a new coffee shop or restaurant or speaking to a new coworker. Once we build positive, new experiences, we can build bigger, more daring experiences for ourselves such as planning a trip to somewhere new or applying to new jobs. But, if we stay with only what makes us comfortable, there's an entire world out there that we're liable to miss. Practice having courage today to try something small but new and, soon, you'll be practicing fearlessness every day.

1. What new thing can you try to step outside of your comfort zone?

_____

_____

_____

_____

_____

_____

_____

2. Describe a time when you were brave and it paid off positively.

_____

_____

_____

_____

_____

_____

_____

day 56

Scared is what you're feeling. Brave is what you're doing.

Emma Donoghue

Bravery doesn't mean we aren't afraid. Bravery is acting even when – especially when – we're scared. Think of the people in your life you think are brave. Do you believe they're never afraid? Of course they experience fear! We often find ourselves envying the bravery and boldness of others because it seems like they're fearless, but we can be brave and bold too. Bravery is an admirable quality, but bravery doesn't mean fearless. Bravery requires fear. If you're fearful, you have the capacity to be brave.

Fear is a feeling we all experience. What we choose to do with fear is what makes us brave or not. Take, for example, the very common experience of being afraid of spiders. It's okay to be afraid of spiders. But if there's a spider in your home that you're afraid of and you choose to remove it yourself, you're demonstrating bravery. Bravery is the act of taking action despite your fears, and if we're fearful, it simply means that we have extra room to demonstrate our bravery.

1. What makes you feel scared?

_____

_____

_____

_____

_____

_____

2. How can you demonstrate bravery in the face of what scares you?

_____

_____

_____

_____

_____

_____

_____

day 57

Trust yourself. You know more than you think.

Benjamin Spock

It's comforting to turn to trusted friends and family to ask for advice or a second opinion. But if you find yourself asking the thoughts and opinions of others about every decision you have, you might not have the confidence in yourself that you deserve. Trust in ourselves comes from experience, and for the most part, we're well-equipped to make our own decisions.

We often know significantly more than we think we do. Whether we're just humble or simply insecure, we didn't get to this point in our lives without being able to think for ourselves. Think of the reason why you're always seeking the opinions and input of others. Is it because you feel safer when your thoughts are backed-up by someone you trust? There are, of course, going to be people in your life who are wiser and more experienced, but you don't always need to seek their advice to make a decision. To practice, try spending a day not asking coworkers or messaging friends or family about your decisions. Decide and plan for yourself and see how it turns out. Chances are, you're more competent and capable of making good decisions than you think you are.

1. What recurring decisions do you always ask for input for? Why?

_____

_____

_____

_____

_____

_____

_____

2. How can you practice making your own informed decisions without outside help?

_____

_____

_____

_____

_____

_____

_____

day 58

I do not believe in taking the right decision, I take a decision and make it right.

Muhammad Ali Jinnah

When we've asked others for their opinions or input on our decisions, we might be afraid to make decisions on our own because we're afraid of making a wrong choice. We want to get the most out of our lives and it makes sense to be afraid of making a mistake, but that all comes down to our perspective. To build a more courageous perspective, change your mindset on what defines a "right" or "wrong" decision.

We have the power to turn what we may think of as a "wrong" decision and make the most out of it. A "wrong" decision is only a differently-imagined "right" decision. And, in the end, we can't change time, so even if a decision we make isn't the "right" one in retrospect, all we can do is work to make it right for us. Changing our perspective will help us be bolder in our decision-making and create a more profound trust in ourselves because if we think that way, we will always make only right decisions. Instead of worrying about what makes a right or wrong decision, focus on which feels right and commit to making it work for you.

1. Is there a decision you're currently worried about making because you're afraid of right or wrong?

_____

_____

_____

_____

_____

_____

_____

2. How can you make it work for you no matter which option you choose?

_____

_____

_____

_____

_____

_____

_____

day 59

Fear defeats more people than any one thing in the world.

Ralph Waldo Emerson

Fear gets in the way of our success and happiness more than any unfortunate circumstances because fear can stop us from taking action. A lack of action keeps us in the same place whether we like it or not. In this way, fear defeats people by stopping their forward momentum. Imagine if fear stopped people from making advances in science and medicine or if people didn't take risks with their art? To take back your forward-moving energy, practice courage and work to manage your fears.

Like we've already talked about, bravery requires fear. If we're fearful, it only means that we have room to demonstrate bravery. Bravery is what pushes people forward in life and propels them to new heights of success and happiness – but it all starts with being afraid. Instead of letting fear paralyze and defeat you, recognize it as the feeling that's in your way and choose to push past it. It's okay to be afraid and it's normal to feel fear, but you have the power to work through it and continue moving forward.

1. In what way has fear defeated you in the past?

_____

_____

_____

_____

_____

_____

2. What are some ways you can encourage yourself to be courageous and take more risks in your life?

_____

_____

_____

_____

_____

_____

_____

day 60

_____ " _____

What would you do if you weren't afraid?

Spencer Johnson

It's a challenging thought, isn't it? What *would* you do if you weren't afraid? It isn't a dare to be reckless, but a challenge to ask you what you feel you're missing out on. Fear can stop us from experiencing pain, but it can also stop us from experiencing joy and excitement. If you're allowing fear to stop you from enjoying your life, think of it as a challenge rather than a roadblock.

Fear doesn't have to stop you. If you want to travel but you're afraid of flying or afraid of getting lost, find a way to make it work. Find alternate ways to travel. or download maps on your phone. If you're afraid of applying for a job, ask yourself – what's the worst that could happen? Fear can paralyze us in ways that stop us from getting more out of life. It's a natural, reasonable feeling that can save us from hardship and heartache, but it doesn't have to rule our lives. Take it as a challenge to summon your courage and try something you've always wanted to do. What's the worst that could happen?

1. What would you do if you weren't afraid?

_____

_____

_____

_____

_____

_____

2. What, besides fear, is stopping you from doing that?

_____

_____

_____

_____

_____

_____

so·bri·e·ty

/səˈbrīədē/

noun

facing problems directly, as opposed to drowning them with fleeting pleasures

day 61

Life is ten percent what you experience and ninety percent
how you respond to it.

Dorothy M. Neddermeyer

It's natural to want to get as much out of life as we possibly can, and for many of us, this means experiencing as much as we can. It's fun and exciting to go out and experience life, but other times life is unavoidably mundane or dull. Fortunately, the power to make an experience – even the dull ones – positive or negative lies entirely with us.

Every experience, whether it's good or bad, is determined by your attitude. What you take away from an experience depends entirely on what you put into it. Our response to our lives is what makes life what it is. People who respond with joy have joyful lives, even if they spend most of their time at work, for example. It's okay to want to experience a lot of life, but remember that how you respond is what makes the experience what it is. You can't always choose what happens to you, but the ability to respond in a way that makes it happy or constructive is up to you.

1. Which unpleasant experiences in your daily life can you change with how you respond to it?

_____

_____

_____

_____

_____

_____

2. How can you change your mindset when you encounter boring or uninteresting experiences?

_____

_____

_____

_____

_____

_____

_____

day 62

———————— " ————————

Happiness is not a matter of intensity but of balance, order, rhythm, and harmony.

Thomas Merton

Happiness means different things to different people. However, we can all find happiness in daily life by accepting our circumstances and choosing to find joy in them. Happiness can be the intense emotions that come with an incredible experience, but those experiences don't happen every day. Instead, we should choose happiness in our daily lives rather than seeking it out in only the best, most exciting experiences.

Happiness can be found everyday as long as we choose to look for it. There's beauty and happiness to be found in how we can count on the sun rising and setting, or in our consistent work, or dependable family members. Our lives have order and rhythm even when it doesn't always feel that way, and this order brings a small, subtle happiness we can choose to look for. Happiness won't always feel intense, and that's okay. Happiness can be loud or soft, but it isn't always one or the other. Learn to look for the quiet, less intense happiness in your everyday life.

1. What are some of the smaller, less intense joys in your life?

_____

_____

_____

_____

_____

_____

_____

2. What can you do to notice and appreciate them more often?

_____

_____

_____

_____

_____

_____

_____

day 63

Speed of life is a killer, not a healer, so slow down and
bloom like a flower.

Debasish Mridha

Have you ever noticed how everyone recommends that we slow down and take it easy when we're feeling unwell? It's sage advice! Slowing down allows our bodies and minds to heal and recharge. When we're constantly on the go, we're not giving ourselves the time or space to reflect and relax. Both are essential to our well-being.

Reflection can be uncomfortable because it can help us process some difficult thoughts or actions. But, just like medicine when you're sick, reflection heals your mind. It isn't possible to avoid negativity or hurt no matter how hard we try. Simply sweeping it under the rug and hurrying off to another event or activity to ignore it only causes it to fester. It isn't good for us to always be in a rush, because when we're in too much of a hurry, we don't have time to sit with our thoughts and feelings. It's true that we have jobs and families and obligations to attend to. There are days when there isn't time to sit down. But when you have the time, make it a priority to slow down, instead of cramming your spare seconds with activities. Slowing down has a healing effect on our minds and bodies. You deserve it.

1. How can you slow down more often in your daily life?

_____

_____

_____

_____

_____

_____

_____

2. When do you notice yourself over-scheduling or overbooking yourself?

_____

_____

_____

_____

_____

_____

_____

day 64

We risk missing out on joy when we get too busy chasing down the extraordinary.

Brenee Brown

Isn't it easy to believe that joy and extraordinary experiences are the same? An extraordinary sunset or an extraordinary trip across the country, or an extraordinarily good cup of coffee can all be joyful, yes. But what about the small, ordinary parts that make up daily life? If you're chasing only the most extraordinary experiences, you're putting yourself into a position to miss out on real, sustainable, everyday joy.

Everyday joy is the ability to find happiness and peace in even the most mundane of tasks. The thousandth sunset you've seen on your commute home has the same potential joy as even the most magnificent sunset in the most scenic place. A cup of regular coffee enjoyed in the quiet morning light can bring the same joy as the best espresso in the finest cafe. Of course, the experiences are different, but they hold the same capacity to be appreciated in the moment for what they are.

If you're only satisfied with the most extraordinary of experiences, you're going to miss out on the joys you can find every day. Take a moment to look around and appreciate the small things in life that bring you joy.

1. What sights, smells, or tastes bring you joy?

_____

_____

_____

_____

_____

_____

2. What routines or rituals can you employ to bring you greater, daily joy?

_____

_____

_____

_____

_____

_____

day 65

Being in a hurry does not slow down time.

Mokokoma Mokhonoana

It certainly feels like rushing through our days gives us more time and room to enjoy ourselves, but what are we missing when we're always in a hurry? No matter how we rush, we only have a limited about of time in a day and, realistically, a limited amount of time in our lives. Rushing may make it feel like we're living life to the fullest, but it's an illusion that causes us to miss out on the quieter, slower parts of life.

To illustrate, think of the last time you were running late for something. You likely hurried out of your home, tried to rush through your commute, and grew frustrated or anxious each time you looked at the clock. But being in a hurry to get somewhere didn't change the time. Our lives work in a similar way. Being in a rush to get to the next exciting event or adventure won't give us more time. To get the most out of life, slow down and notice your surroundings, take in the details, and don't hurry past the experiences that make life beautiful and worthwhile.

1. Which parts of your life do you rush through?

_____

_____

_____

_____

_____

_____

2. How can you practice slowing down and taking notice of even the ordinary parts of life?

_____

_____

_____

_____

_____

_____

_____

day 66

"

Many people lose the small joys in the hope for the big happiness.

Pearl S. Buck

We all want happiness, of course, but we have different ideas and expectations of what that is. Some people are content with the small joys in life, but others miss out in their pursuit for something bigger and better. If we are always pursuing bigger, better happiness, we risk missing out on smaller, perhaps more sustainable happiness all along the way.

To move away from pursuing "the big happiness," we should practice slowing down and appreciating the small joys. Contentment is an invaluable trait that we can all stand to develop. Contentment requires us to be satisfied with what we have in our lives without desiring more. When we are content, we enjoy what already exists in our life and what's already available to us. It doesn't mean we shouldn't have goals or ambitions, but we should also enjoy what we have at the time. Contentment will bring us ease, calm, and the sobriety required to enjoy the big and small happiness in our lives. It's okay to want "the big happiness," but don't miss out on the small ones along the way.

1. List some of the small parts of your life that bring you happiness.

_____

_____

_____

_____

_____

_____

2. How can you practice contentment while still having goals?

_____

_____

_____

_____

_____

_____

_____

day 67

Knowing how to be solitary is central to the art of loving.
When we can be alone, we can be with others without
using them as a means of escape.

Bell Hooks

When we're feeling bad, it's easy to choose to spend time with people who make us feel good. It's wonderful to have friends who can comfort us and cheer us up, but there's a difference between going to friends for comfort and using them for escape.

When we're escaping our negative feelings, we're avoiding talking about or acknowledging them. Using people as an escape means you depend on their positivity and energy to drown out your own negative feelings. Going to them for comfort means seeking support and guidance. Learning to be solitary forces you to sit with your emotions and acknowledge them. When we've learned to accept solitude, we can depend on ourselves to handle our emotions instead of hoping our friends will hide us from them. Learn to handle your uncomfortable emotions so that you can process them in a healthy manner, and find joy in people for who they are, rather than what they shield you from.

1. How can you practice giving yourself more space to experience solitude?

_____

_____

_____

_____

_____

_____

_____

2. How can you make solitude more appealing to yourself?

_____

_____

_____

_____

_____

_____

_____

day 68

For after all, the best thing one can do when it rains is to let it rain.

Henry Wadsworth Longfellow

No one enjoys experiencing pain and hardship, but both are unavoidable parts of life. How we respond to hardship determines how we come out of it and, often, how quickly. The reality is that we can't outrun unpleasant feelings or situations forever and eventually they're bound to catch up with us. Like Longfellow says, the best thing we can do is to let it rain. This means that the best action we can take when life is difficult is confrontation rather than avoidance.

Avoiding problems or unpleasantry is only a temporary bandage and, in some cases, hardships only get harder if left unattended to. Confronting unpleasant feelings or situations as they arise gives us the freedom to move forward more quickly. It isn't enjoyable and it certainly isn't always easy, but like the rain, it doesn't last forever. Practice giving immediate attention to unpleasantry to help you become more balanced and present.

1. How do you find yourself avoiding unpleasant situations in your life?

_____

_____

_____

_____

_____

_____

2. What are some steps you can take to prioritize problems as they arise rather than putting them off or playing them down?

_____

_____

_____

_____

_____

_____

_____

day 69

Do not spoil what you have by desiring what you have not.

Ann Brashares

Gratitude is a nice idea, but it isn't always easy in practice. Our lives are filled with inescapable images of beautiful clothes, fun vacations, or other nice items or experiences that we may want. It isn't unhealthy that we want nice things or exciting experiences, but the act of being unappreciative of what we have is unhealthy. A lack of gratitude breeds resentment and makes what we already have seem lackluster.

To practice being grateful, keep track of what you're thankful for. A boring birthday party might not be what you want to be doing when you know you could be out doing something more exciting, but think about what you're celebrating and who you're celebrating with! It's wonderful to celebrate the life of another person. Your shoes might not be designer, but they protect your feet every day. Your trip might not be "instagramable" but it's nice to get away and experience new things. It's okay to want nice, exciting things. But don't let your desire for them ruin what you already have. Practice gratitude and watch how your contentment grows.

1. What in your life are you grateful for?

_____

_____

_____

_____

_____

_____

2. How can you practice gratitude in your daily life?
Journaling? Sharing with others?

_____

_____

_____

_____

_____

_____

_____

_____"_____

Nothing is as powerful as allowing yourself to be truly
affected by things.

Zooey Deschanel

Running from negativity isn't sustainable. It can feel like we're in control when we choose to be positive or engage in fun or exciting behavior, instead of allowing ourselves to feel bad. But we're giving up an important power when we choose to run from negativity: the power to feel. If you allow yourself to only feel fun, happy feelings, you're limiting your emotional range.

Real power lies in our ability to feel and express our feelings, even the bad ones. To allow yourself to feel sadness, shame, and guilt is a growing opportunity. It expands your emotional range and intelligence and builds resilience. So, the next time something sad or frustrating happens, you'll be better equipped to handle it. The next time you're tempted to drown out negative emotions with fun experiences, pause. Remind yourself that it's normal to feel bad sometimes and that it's a step toward being stronger next time. It might not feel like it right away, but allowing yourself to feel all of your emotions will benefit you in the long run.

1. Describe a time when you drowned out a negative feeling.

_____

_____

_____

_____

_____

_____

_____

2. How can you slow down and allow yourself to experience all of your emotions?

_____

_____

_____

_____

_____

_____

_____

days 71 -80

---

in·no·cence

/ˈinəsəns/

noun

experiencing life the way a child does: seeing circumstances as they are without needing to control them

---

Days 71-80 • Enneagram 8 • Innocence

day 71

In a gentle way, you can shake the world.

Mahatma Gandhi

It seems unlikely that gentleness should be able to get us anywhere in the world. Especially when news and media bombards us with loud, angry people, with louder, angrier messages. However, many of the greatest leaders and activists in history have been peaceful, gentle people with strong, ambitious agendas. We can learn from the powerful actions of gentle people that we don't need to embrace the loud, angry way of the world in order to change it.

Self-empowerment doesn't necessarily look like anger and aggression. In fact, self-empowerment can be compassionate and self-confident without being domineering. When we're confident in ourselves and passionate about our cares and causes, we can be inspiring. Innocence in action and behavior doesn't mean that we aren't direct or timid, it means that we're calm and gentle while maintaining our strong, resilient nature. To move toward innocence, notice when your behavior might be tipping toward aggressive or domineering actions, and take action to be more gentle. Gentleness speaks volumes louder than anger.

1. In which ways are your words or actions loud or angry?

_____

_____

_____

_____

_____

_____

2. How can you modify your loud actions to be softer but still assertive?

_____

_____

_____

_____

_____

_____

_____

day 72

Remain calm, serene, always in command of yourself. You will then find out how easy it is to get along.

Paramahansa Yogananda

It can be difficult to get along with people. Everyone has different ideas, values, opinions, and preferences and, when we all have to work and live together, we can end up clashing. But we don't have to succumb to discomfort or conflict. Instead of choosing to be confrontational, we can choose to be calm and serene and allow others their differences.

We can allow others to have their differences without giving up our own values and certainly without sacrificing what we believe is right and true. Like we learned yesterday, we can approach the world with gentleness and serenity and still uphold our strong values and agendas. When we speak and act gently despite our differences with others, it's amazing how easily we can get along with them while maintaining our values. Being calm and serene won't make you vulnerable to others controlling or taking advantage of you, it simply means that you are calmly and powerfully in control of yourself. When you're calmly in control, you'll notice that others are easy to get along with.

1. How can you practice being calm and serene even when you're experiencing differences with other people?

_____

_____

_____

_____

_____

_____

2. How can you be gentle while maintaining your values?

_____

_____

_____

_____

_____

_____

day 73

Keep cool. Anger is not an argument.

Daniel Webster

Sometimes it seems that whoever is louder and angrier is the stronger voice in an argument. Argument and conflict is a healthy and normal part of life. Without argument, we wouldn't experience change or resolve differences. With that in mind, it's also important to note that we can engage in conflict without demonstrating anger or aggression. When we keep a cool, level head, we have a better chance of opening the doors of communication and understanding.

Anger itself isn't a bad thing. But it isn't, as Daniel Webster says, an argument. Reacting to an argument in anger demonstrates how you feel, but it could also communicate that you're unwilling to have an open discussion or that you're unwilling to compromise. The point of an argument is to express clearly how you feel and move to resolve an issue. It's okay to be angry, but make sure your arguments also communicate your desire to reach a resolution instead of trying to "win." Sometimes we're unaware of how strong we come off in an argument. Make it a point to be approachable and cool when conflict arises so you can move toward resolution quickly and effectively. Anger and conflict are inevitable, but we're capable of engaging with one without expressing the other.

1. What actions can you take to keep cool in a disagreement?

_____

_____

_____

_____

_____

_____

2. How can you express your anger or frustration without being loud or aggressive?

_____

_____

_____

_____

_____

_____

_____

_____ " _____

We are at our most powerful the moment we no longer
need to be powerful.

Eric Micha'el Leventhal

Vulnerability is an incredible measure of our courage. It takes strength and bravery to demonstrate vulnerability, even to the people we love and trust. Always being strong may make us feel powerful, but power also lies in the ability to let down our walls and share ourselves with others. Vulnerability is not synonymous with weakness any more than being closed-off is synonymous with being powerful.

When we experience vulnerability, we're opening ourselves up to strong, human emotions and allowing others to experience them with us. It isn't always easy and it certainly isn't always comfortable, but it can open new avenues of thought and creation. Vulnerability allows you to experience empathy, and it can hurt. But the question that's bound to stop you from growing and living a full life is "what should I be afraid of?" When we're afraid of letting go of our power, we're letting go of experiencing broader, stronger emotions and deeper relationships. Taking steps to stop being strong and powerful, even if it's limited to certain times with certain people, will give you more power than you ever imagined.

1. Who do you trust enough to be vulnerable with?

_____

_____

_____

_____

_____

_____

_____

2. Which "soft" feelings are you worried about showing to others? Why?

_____

_____

_____

_____

_____

_____

_____

day 75

> Your suffering needs to be respected. Don't try to ignore the hurt, because it is real. Just let the hurt soften you instead of hardening you. Let the hurt open you instead of closing you. Let the hurt send you looking for those who will accept you instead of hiding from those who reject you.
>
> Bryant McGill

It's tempting to allow hurt to harden us as a way to protect ourselves from future pain. But when we close ourselves off and let pain harden our hearts, we're also barring ourselves from experiencing deep love and trust from others. Instead of putting up walls when something or someone hurts you, acknowledge the pain and seek comfort from those who won't.

We can experience love and trust only so long as we open ourselves up to it. Softness doesn't make us targets, just as emotional walls don't protect just from hurt. There are people in your life who are willing to love and care for you if you'll open yourself to it. Don't let a few bad experiences stop you from experiencing a wealth of emotions and human connections. You deserve to experience the softer side of life.

1. Which experiences in your life caused you to build walls?

_____

_____

_____

_____

_____

_____

2. How can you choose to be open rather than hardening with hurt?

_____

_____

_____

_____

_____

_____

day 76

To share your weakness is to make yourself vulnerable; to make yourself vulnerable is to show your strength.

Criss Jami

All of us have weaknesses, whether we share them with others or not. Sharing our weaknesses can be frightening because it's possible that other people will want to take advantage of us. But, more often than not, sharing our weaknesses helps others come alongside us instead of creating an opportunity for people to hurt us.

It takes bravery to make ourselves vulnerable. By some definitions, vulnerability is a weak point our enemies can attack. For us, vulnerability simply means sharing our weaknesses so others can better see and assist us. Showing others that we also fall short and experience fear or grief is showing others that we're relatable. Everyone experiences difficulty and it's easier when we can share in one another's pain and suffering. There's strength in ourselves, but there's also strength in numbers. Don't allow your pride or your fear to push others away when your burden can be shared. By showing ourselves in our weakest, most vulnerable states, we're inviting others to see our strength. Everyone experiences pain, but it takes strength for someone to share it.

1. In what ways can you share your weaknesses with others you trust?

_____

_____

_____

_____

_____

_____

2. How do you come alongside people who are hurting and showing weakness?

_____

_____

_____

_____

_____

_____

"

People can be at their most vulnerable, but still tenacious at the same time.

Toni Bernhard

Vulnerability isn't weak. Vulnerability can actually be the most powerful tool at our disposal. When we're showing our true, open selves, we're also showing what we care passionately about. Showing what you care about can only lead to you demonstrating what you care about. Being openly passionate is what prompts us to fight for change in our lives and the world around us. Think about the biggest concerns in your life right now. Don't you want others to feel strongly about them as well? Be the change you want to see and share with others how you feel.

If you care about a cause, you might feel strong emotions about it. It could be anger, but it could also be profound sadness or hurt. If you show others these softer, more tender emotions, you have the opportunity to share what breaks your heart with others. Mobilizing others to follow your lead or commit to causes starts with relatable, powerful thoughts and feelings. You have the power, by sharing your vulnerability, to move others. Vulnerability won't stop you. You can be intensely vulnerable and intensely strong and powerful all at the same time.

1. What concerns in your life cause powerful, tender emotions?

_____

_____

_____

_____

_____

_____

_____

2. How might others join your fight if you share your vulnerability with them?

_____

_____

_____

_____

_____

_____

_____

"

Lead from the back and let others think they're in front.

Nelson Mandela

If we have strong ideas, opinions, and leadership skills, we want to employ them. Those of us who are confident in ourselves and our skills are natural-born leaders. However, if we're too confident, we might be perceived as pushy or aggressive. Neither of those attributes are particularly well-received in a respected leader, so how can we lead from the back as Nelson Mandela did?

Practice giving others in your life or on your team some responsibility. You don't have to do every piece of a task on your own, no matter how good you are at it. Effective leadership requires us to delegate tasks and let others have autonomy. Build others up so that they can work in their own way. Allow others the space to work on their own without inserting yourself. Strong leaders also have strong people behind them. Build people up and make sure everyone has the same autonomy that you crave.

1. How can you delegate tasks in your life?

_____

_____

_____

_____

_____

_____

2. What can we do or say to build others up?

_____

_____

_____

_____

_____

_____

_____

day 79

The strongest and most courageous of us all is the one with an open heart.

Maria Koszler

We often think of open-hearted individuals as tender, breakable, and maybe even subordinate. There's nothing wrong with any of those traits, but there's also nothing wrong with being tender-hearted. Additionally, that isn't to say that bold, independent people can't also be open-hearted. In fact, some of the strongest and most courageous people in history have had open hearts. Activists, world leaders, and philanthropists have all had compassionate, loving hearts while maintaining their ambition and passion.

The people we see as tender-hearted are often the same people who are out in the world fighting to make a difference. Can you imagine if we all, with our strength and passion, allowed ourselves to open our hearts and worked to ignite change? We all have the capability to have a soft heart – no matter how hard we have to work to make it so. And when our hearts are open to others, we are open to gaining love and understanding, too. Having your heart out for others isn't easy, but it's strong and courageous. If we allow ourselves, we can be vulnerable and open-hearted.

1. Who is someone with an open heart who you admire?

_____

_____

_____

_____

_____

_____

2. How can you become more open-hearted in your daily life?

_____

_____

_____

_____

_____

_____

_____ " _____

When you protect yourself from pain, be sure not to protect yourself from love.

Alan Cohen

When we experience pain, we try to avoid experiencing it in the same way again. It's a learning process. A small child won't touch a hot stove twice, for example. Emotional pain is no different. When we experience emotional pain, we try to learn from the experience so we don't repeat it. However, some of us choose to emotionally close ourselves off rather than trying to find new ways to love. For some of us, we try to protect ourselves from not allowing any tender emotions to reach the surface.

Closing our softer emotions off works to a certain extent. Certainly it's harder to hurt us if we're not allowing others to influence our feelings. But if we're shutting others out to protect ourselves from pain, we're also closing ourselves off from love. The reality is that we're human and we will experience hurt, but we're also capable of experiencing love at the same time. Instead of shutting others out to protect ourselves from pain, let's practice opening ourselves to love. If you're going to love, you're going to hurt, but, if you let yourself, you can also experience the comfort, healing, and security of love.

1. Describe an experience that made you shut others out.

_____

_____

_____

_____

_____

_____

2. How do you prefer to be loved? (Kind words, kind gestures, quality time, etc.)

_____

_____

_____

_____

_____

_____

_____

days 81 - 90

---

ac·tion

/ˈakSH(ə)n/

noun

the fact or process of doing
something to achieve an aim

Days 81-90 • Enneagram 9 • Action

187

day 81

People often say that motivation doesn't last. Well, neither does bathing. That's why we recommend it daily.

Zig Ziglar

No one, not even the most energetic of us, can reasonably expect to always have motivation. It's common to get excited about a project or event and to spend time and energy on it until your motivation runs out. If you're someone who has many unfinished projects, you need to work on your motivation.

We don't just "get" motivation-we have to work for it. We have to wake up every day and set intentions. If we depend on a spark of energy or inspiration to move us, we'll never finish anything. Instead of starting a project when you're motivated and stopping it when you aren't, make a commitment to yourself. It doesn't feel very good to have unfinished projects, so make a plan to finish one no matter how motivated you feel. Tell yourself each day that you're going to spend time on the project and, little by little, you'll start completing the projects. Motivation isn't something we can maintain over long periods of time. Energy comes and goes, but we can always move forward, even when we're not feeling like it.

1. What are some words or mantras you can develop to give yourself daily motivation?

_____

_____

_____

_____

_____

_____

_____

2. How can you set aside your distractions to prioritize what really needs to be done?

_____

_____

_____

_____

_____

_____

_____

day 82

Action is a great restorer and builder of confidence.
Inaction is not only the result but the cause, of fear.

Norman Vincent Peale

Numbing the world around us can make us feel disconnected and possibly less stressed. But it will certainly cause us to not take action, which will sow doubt in our mind and may make us want to numb ourselves again. Inaction and pulling away from a stressful world is a vicious cycle, but it can be broken. If we summon our courage, we can move forward to break the cycle of inaction and fear.

We live in a world with a lot of demands, pressures, and stresses. They're unavoidable, but what you do with your stress and how you handle it changes everything. If you go home at the end of the day with no intention or motivation to make things better for yourself, everything will stay the same. Taking action isn't without risk but where there's potential risk, there's potential reward. If we step outside of our comfort zones, stop escaping the stresses of our lives, and confront them head-on, we can build confidence and courage in ourselves. Life is stressful, but we don't have to sit back and let it happen to us. Let's go out and make it work for us.

1. What are some actions you can take today to make your life easier or more pleasant?

_____

_____

_____

_____

_____

_____

_____

2. What activities do you engage in to tune out from the world instead of confronting your stress?

_____

_____

_____

_____

_____

_____

_____

day 83

Inaction breeds doubts and fears. Action breeds confidence and courage. If you want to conquer fear, do not sit at home and think about it. Go out and get busy.

Dale Carnegie

Inaction can feel comfortable. If you don't act, nothing changes. Your relationships, jobs, and hobbies stay the same and will never be the cause of conflict. However, inaction can quietly grow anxiety and discontent. If you're unhappy in your relationships or job, not taking action to make meaningful changes will grow that discontent. If you're allowing your unhappiness to grow by keeping things as they are, be bold and think about what you want and need.

Instead of being fearful that making changes will cause conflict and discomfort, recognize that taking action will improve your life more than it will hurt you. Asking for what you want and deserve will build your confidence because you'll be investing in yourself. Taking action to improve yourself and your circumstances will teach you your own value and teach others how to treat you. It's always easier said than done. But, with practice, you'll be able to build the confidence and courage to take action for yourself and your needs.

1. What parts of your life are causing you discontent?

_____

_____

_____

_____

_____

_____

_____

2. What do you want or need to improve those parts of your life?

_____

_____

_____

_____

_____

_____

_____

day 84

Responsibility to yourself means refusing to let others do your thinking, talking, and naming for you; it means learning to respect and use your own brains and instincts; hence, grappling with hard work.

Adreinne Rich

It's too easy to allow others to think and talk for us. But we're all capable, intelligent individuals with our own minds and we all deserve to use and speak them. Not only do we deserve to use our own minds, we have a responsibility to ourselves to respect our own voice and opinions. If we've been in a pattern of allowing others to speak for us, it can be upsetting to ourselves and others when we develop our own voice. However, it's respectful to ourselves and to others to speak our own minds.

To work toward speaking for ourselves, we need to accept that it isn't always easy. "Going with the flow" has historically led to a lack of conflict, but it isn't always responsible. It's hard work to speak our minds, but when we do, we're demonstrating our own birthright of autonomy and self-respect, and giving the rest of the world what it deserves: your voice. Even if it isn't saying what everyone wants to hear.

1. When was the last time you allowed yourself to speak out against what others were saying?

_____

_____

_____

_____

_____

_____

_____

2. What does being responsible to yourself look like to you?

_____

_____

_____

_____

_____

_____

_____

day 85

Find something you're passionate about and keep
tremendously interested in it.

Julia Child

Sometimes it's easier to absorb the interests of the people around us. Choosing to be interested in the same games or hobbies as others is an easy way to make friends, but it stops us from finding what we ourselves are passionate about. Sometimes it can even be frightening to develop and show our own true passions because we wonder what others will think. Rather than choosing to have the same interests as your friends or family because it's convenient, take some time to find what you're passionate about.

Cultivating and practicing our own passions helps us build the confidence and courage to be ourselves. Imagine if Julia Child or Thelonious Monk hadn't pursued their passions for food or music! We're happiest when we're working on the projects and interests that we care about the most. You deserve to find your passion and to develop it. Build your own interests and set your own course – it's worth it.

1. Are there hobbies or interests you've developed out of convenience rather than true interest?

_____

_____

_____

_____

_____

_____

2. How can you discover your own passions?

_____

_____

_____

_____

_____

_____

_____

"

> It were not best that we should all think alike; it is
> difference of opinion that makes horse races.
>
> Mark Twain

Disagreement isn't necessarily easy, but it's necessary. Can you imagine a world where we all thought the same thing? There wouldn't be any creativity or innovation. A balance of agreeing and disagreeing is what makes the world around us grow and change. But don't make the mistake that a difference of opinion has to mean an argument. Conflict is unavoidable, but it doesn't have to mean that each time you voice a different thought that there will be conflict. Sometimes, giving voice to your own thoughts is nothing more than a few words for someone else to consider.

It's okay to voice your thoughts and opinions even when they're different from those you love and admire. When we disagree, it opens the opportunity for discussion and debate, which can lead to growth and increased understanding. It truly isn't best that we should all think alike. Difference of opinion is what makes us grow. Don't stunt your growth by choosing to think like others, or by remaining silent when you have different thoughts.

1. Describe a time when you had a different opinion but preferred to keep quiet. Why did you make that choice?

_____

_____

_____

_____

_____

_____

2. Who in your life do you feel safe voicing different opinions to?

_____

_____

_____

_____

_____

_____

day 87

_____ " _____

Be who you are and say what you feel because those who matter won't mind and those who mind don't matter.

Bernard Baruch

When we begin to develop our voices and individual thoughts and opinions, some people may push back. If we've spent time going with the flow to avoid conflict or inconvenience, it may come as a surprise to others when you begin taking action for yourself. Some may be proud of you for being yourself, and others may be frustrated that you're not as malleable as you used to be. Fortunately, this uncomfortable position makes it easy to see who matters and who doesn't.

The people in your life who want what's best for you will be happy to see you taking action, making your own decisions, and having your own thoughts. They want you to be an individual and they won't mind when you are yourself. There are others, however, in our lives who may wish for us to remain inactive because we're easier to control or manipulate when we're not secure enough to voice our own decisions. These people will mind that you're more vocal, but they are the people who don't matter. Developing your voice isn't easy because you will almost certainly upset some people, but they'll help you see who has your best interests at heart.

1. In which ways are you slow to be yourself because you're afraid of what others with think?

_____

_____

_____

_____

_____

_____

_____

2. Is there a specific event in your daily life where you can begin voicing your opinion?

_____

_____

_____

_____

_____

_____

_____

day 88

Don't be afraid to speak your mind. You have one for a reason.

Sarah Moores

You are an intelligent, independent individual with a working heart and mind, and you, just as much as anyone else, deserve to use it. No one has any more right than you do to voice their thoughts and opinions. You, just as much as anyone else, have a mind. If you don't speak up, no one will know what you're thinking or feeling. And, in some cases, not speaking your mind will allow the spread of bad ideas or information.

The world has seen the catastrophic results of large numbers of people not speaking their mind. In many cases, speaking your mind is the right thing to do. It can provide insight, challenge false arguments, or simply provide another thought or opinion. We're equipped with minds so that we can communicate. We aren't just able to communicate – it's our responsibility to do so. It's our responsibility to speak up when we hear false information or hear slanderous talk. You have a powerful mind that knows what's right and what's wrong. Don't allow yourself to shirk your responsibility to speak your mind.

1. Describe a time when you were afraid to speak your mind.

_____

_____

_____

_____

_____

_____

2. Describe a time when speaking your mind was the responsible thing to do. Did you speak up?

_____

_____

_____

_____

_____

_____

day 89

_____ " _____

It took me quite a long time to develop a voice, and now that I have it, I am not going to be silent.

Madeleine K. Albright

We all have different voices. Your voice is whatever you use to communicate your thoughts and ideas. It can be spoken, signed, painted, or danced. No matter how we choose to communicate, once we've developed a way, we're never going to want to give it up. That's how meaningful our voices are – once we have it, we won't want to be silent.

To develop your voice, simply practice speaking up. When someone asks for your opinion, give it to them. If you're asked about the movie you want to watch, where you want to eat dinner, or what you want to do on Friday night, tell them. It starts small. When you're more comfortable saying what you want, you can start talking about how you feel. Eventually you'll be able to speak confidently for yourself and for others. You are your own advocate. Once you realize the power of speaking up for yourself, you'll never look back.

1. Describe a time when you agreed to something because it's what you thought someone else wanted.

_____

_____

_____

_____

_____

_____

_____

2. How will you respond the next time someone asks your opinion?

_____

_____

_____

_____

_____

_____

_____

day 90

Let today mark a new beginning for you. Give yourself permission to say NO without feeling guilty, mean, or selfish. Anybody who gets upset and/or expects you to say YES all of the time clearly doesn't have your best interest at heart. Always remember: You have a right to say NO without having to explain yourself. Be at peace with your decisions.

Stephanie Lahart

Today is the day you begin advocating for yourself and developing your voice. You might upset some people along the way, but that will tell you who cares about you and who doesn't. Developing your voice when you've been hesitant to speak up is a long, powerful journey. But in the end, your voice will be your own and everyone will respect that. In a world where so many other people are giving voice to their thoughts, why shouldn't you?

There's nothing wrong or mean about speaking your mind – as long as it's done in a caring and loving way – and, for the most part, people will understand that. It's okay to disagree and offer alternative views. People want to hear what you have to say. The people in your life truly care about what you think and feel. Don't make anyone guess what you're thinking any longer. You have a powerful, beautiful voice. Use it!

1. How can you speak your mind today?

_____

_____

_____

_____

_____

_____

2. Who in your life clearly has your best interests at heart?

_____

_____

_____

_____

_____

_____

_____

Conclusion: What's Next?

You have been taking this journey slow and steady, one step at a time, day-by-day. When you make small, incremental change, it's sometimes difficult to notice the profound changes that are happening in the amount of harmony, joy, and mental clarity you carry with you each day. Take some time to reflect on who you were three months ago. Consider how you felt about yourself, the people around you, your job, and your hobbies. Think about how much joy you received from the simple things in life, and how you reacted to the stressful things in life. Write down the qualities you remember about yourself of three months ago:

_____

_____

_____

_____

_____

Now, think about yourself today. Think about how differently you approach the world now that you have the wisdom of the Enneagram on your side. Think about the remarkable changes you made in your serenity, humility, authenticity, equanimity, non-attachment, courage, sobriety, innocence, and action. Write down the changes you notice in yourself:

_____

_____

_____

_____

_____

Today, you are a new person. And guess what? It doesn't end here. Even if you never devote time to your self-development ever again, you will still reap the benefits of a newly-formed growth mindset. This means that you have proven to yourself that with a little bit of effort, you can achieve anything – even down to reshaping your limiting beliefs, harmful thought patterns, and behavioral habits. Not only do you know intellectually that you can do or become "anything you want," but you've proven it to yourself. No one can take that away from you now. You are a new person.

We, of course, recommend that you **do** continue devoting time to your self-development. Why? Because we think you'll reap the most benefits if you continue testing just how much harmony, joy, and mental clarity you can squeeze out of life.

Personally, we love using the Enneagram as our tool of choice for continual psychological growth. The Enneagram is simple enough to be boiled down to a list of nine personalities, but it can be explored more deeply for a lifetime's worth of wisdom and knowledge to guide a person to their best and most fulfilled life.

For more resources to learn about the Enneagram and how it can further improve your life, read the rest of our Enneagram series, which can be found at www.personalityintel.com. However, you already have a powerful set of tools right here. When you find yourself needing more courage, head back to the courage block and spend 10 days refreshing your knowledge of how you can melt away fear. If you notice that things are feeling overly chaotic and you need another dose of serenity, re-do the serenity block to replenish your stores of inner peace. Each time you revisit a section, you are strengthening new pathways you formed over the last 90 days. We suggest you revisit them often.

You are also walking away with nine powerful meditations that you can continue to use weekly to deeply instill each of the nine virtues into your core. We still do one of the nine meditations each morning, because 1) waking up to any type of mindfulness has momentous effects that are both mental *and* physical. It truly is incredible. And 2) mindfulness centered on the Enneagram virtues, specifically, grounds us in the most crucial philosophies and psychological principles that we all so desperately need for a fulfilled life, but are so starved of in modern day times. Take a break, because you've done a lot to be proud of over the last 90 days. But when you're ready, consider challenging yourself to nine consecutive days of meditation and see how it helps you feel simultaneously lighter and more grounded.

You may have heard the saying: "you are the average of the five people you spend your time with" or "show me your friends and I'll show you who you are" or "birds of a feather flock together." Clichés are clichés for a reason, and there is some deep and significant truth to this one.

Who are the five people you spend the most time with?

1. _____

2. _____

3. _____

4. _____

5. _____

Evaluate the list you wrote above and make sure you are devoting significant time to relationships that make you better, not relationships that limit your potential. The one thing that can hamper your journey of self-growth is surrounding yourself with people who seem to prefer the nine vices over the nine virtues. There are a few things you can do to make sure you have mostly positive influences around you: 1) limit negative social media, 2) find and utilize positive connections, and 3) encourage your loved ones to embark on their own Enneagram journey.

In this arena, technology is both a blessing and a curse. Social media surrounds us with a constant feed of negative and/or trivial information. However, on the flip side, we can now connect with any positive influence regardless of where it may be in the world. We can watch videos and read content from people who are achieving the goals we want to achieve. We can virtually surround ourselves with people we want to be the average of. Make technology your friend, not your enemy, in this arena.

Think critically about your social media usage. Is it feeding you more of the nine virtues or more of the nine vices?

_____

_____

_____

How can you use social media for even more positive influence?

_____

_____

_____

For the people in your life who are close to you, gift them with wisdom of the Enneagram to increase their harmony, joy, and mental clarity, and also to foster an environment of growth within your social circle. If your friends are happier and healthier, you will be too. Serenity, humility, authenticity, equanimity, non-attachment, courage, sobriety, innocence, and action can ripple through your circle, starting with you.

Gift a copy of this book to five friends who seem ready to transform their lives and see how the impact ripples outward from there. This is a suggestion that may seem like it benefits us. Frankly, it does. Our mission in life is impact, and we choose to make that impact by teaching as many people as possible how they can use the Enneagram to take control of their lives. Ultimately, though, you will reap the most reward. If you find you are losing your sense of authenticity, for example, it will be far easier to gain it back if your loved ones are also practiced in authenticity. Compare that to a situation where you are constantly surrounded by subtle patterns of deceit, envy, and other harmful vices. This, of course, will unnecessarily complicate your own growth. Share the wisdom you've gained to help others benefit from harmony, joy and mental clarity, and simultaneously amplify your own. Without you, they may never hear about or learn these principles. You could be the start of an enduring ripple.

Last but not least, let's take a moment to celebrate you. Committing to something for 90 days is simple – but it isn't easy. You, however, made the choice to devote time to your growth and progress each day and have proven to yourself that you can do something that challenges your status quo, stretches your mind, and demands more from your life and your capabilities. Be proud of yourself. Remember the treat you promised yourself back when we first started this journey together? Don't forget to follow through on that as well. If your preferences have changed over the 90 days and you'd prefer a different treat, that's okay. But make sure you are intentional about keeping your word to reward yourself for a job well done, the same way you would keep a promise you made to anyone else. Let's set an intention right here and right now. What is your treat for finishing this 90-day journey and when will you gift it to yourself? Write out the following on the lines below:

For completing this 90-day journey I will treat myself with <<promise to yourself>> <<when and where>>.

_____

_____

_____

_____

_____

_____

_____

We are proud of you. And you should be too! If you haven't already connected with us, please do. We would love to hear how your 90-day journey went, what you have in mind for next steps, or answer any questions you may have about the Enneagram and how to use it to improve your life. We can be reached at jjsanders@personalityintel.com and we would absolutely love to hear from you.

With love,

Jody Sanders

Jeff Sanders

Jody and Jeff Sanders
www.personalityintel.com
jjsanders@personalityintel.com

Made in the USA
Monee, IL
21 April 2020

26138148R10118